GOD'S STORY AND
MODERN LITERATURE

GOD'S STORY AND MODERN LITERATURE

Reading Fiction in Community

CARL FICKEN

FORTRESS PRESS   Philadelphia

Library of Congress Cataloging in Publication Data

Ficken, Carl.
  God's story and modern literature.

  Includes bibliographical references.
    1. American fiction—20th century—History and criticism. 2. Religion in literature. 3. Christianity in literature. 4. Theology in literature. 5. American fiction—Southern States—History and criticism.
I. Title.
PS374.R47F53 1985   813'.5'09382   84–48705
ISBN 0–8006–1823–8

1251B85   Printed in the United States of America   1–1823

CONTENTS

ACKNOWLEDGMENTS

Excerpt from *Bloodline* by Ernest Gaines. Copyright © 1964 by Ernest Gaines. Reprinted by permission of Doubleday & Co., Inc. A Dial Press Book.

Excerpt from *The Autobiography of Miss Jane Pittman* by Ernest Gaines. Copyright © 1971 by Ernest J. Gaines. A Dial Press Book. Reprinted by permission of Doubleday & Co., Inc.

Reynolds Price, excerpt from "A Chain of Love" in *The Names and Faces of Heroes*. Copyright © 1962 by Reynolds Price. Reprinted with the permission of Atheneum publishers.

Reynolds Price, excerpt from *A Palpable God*. Copyright © 1978 by Reynolds Price. Reprinted with the permission of Atheneum publishers.

Excerpts from *Interviews with Black Writers* by John O'Brien, by permission of Liveright Publishing Corporation. Copyright © 1973 by Liveright Publishing Corporation.

Excerpts from *Mystery and Manners* by Flannery O'Connor. Edited by Sally and Robert Fitzgerald. Copyright © 1957, 1961, 1963, 1964, 1966, 1967, 1969 by the Estate of Mary Flannery O'Connor. Reprinted by permission of Farrar, Straus & Giroux, Inc.

Excerpts from *The Habit of Being* by Flannery O'Connor. Edited by Sally Fitzgerald. Copyright © 1979 by Regina O'Connor. Reprinted by permission of Farrar, Straus & Giroux, Inc.

Excerpts from "Parker's Back" from *The Complete Stories by Flan-nery O'Connor.* Copyright © 1965, 1971 by the Estate of Mary Flannery O'Connor. Reprinted by permission of Farrar, Straus & Giroux, Inc.

Excerpts from *Lion in the Garden: Interviews with William Faulkner 1926–62* by James Meriwether and Michael Millgate. Copyright © 1968 by Michael Millgate. Reprinted by permission of Michael Millgate.

Excerpt from *Faulkner in the University: Class Conferences at the University of Virginia, 1957–58,* ed. by Frederick L. Gwynn and Joseph L. Blotner. Copyright © 1965 by University Press of Virginia. Reprinted by permission of The University Press of Virginia.

Excerpt from *Light in August* by William Faulkner. Copyright © 1968 by Random House, Inc. Copyright © 1932 by William Faulkner. Copyright renewed 1959 by William Faulkner. Reprinted by permis-sion of Random House, Inc.

Excerpt from *Collected Stories of William Faulkner* by William Faulkner. Copyright, 1934, 1950, by Random House, Inc. Copyright, 1935 by William Faulkner. Reprinted by permission of Random House, Inc.

Excerpts from *In Search of Our Mother's Gardens* by Alice Walker are reprinted by permission of the publisher, Harcourt Brace Jovanovich, Inc.

PREFACE

One of Flannery O'Connor's most interesting characters is O. E. Parker, a man with tattoos all over his body. Parker had seen a tattooed man at a fair, had been impressed by the beauty and harmony of those pictures, and had begun, at the age of fifteen, to cover his own body with tattoos, hoping for a satisfying sense of wholeness. When Parker met Sarah Ruth Cates, a woman who was "plain, plain," he married her despite her plainness, her apparent disinterest in his tattoos, and her rather eager Christian commitment (her father was a "Straight Gospel preacher" who was "away, spreading it in Florida"). In hopes of pleasing her, Parker has a picture of God—actually, a Byzantine Christ—tattooed on his back, the last free space he has. Convinced that God is a "spirit" and that pictures are idolatry, however, she beats Parker's back until welts come on the face of Christ. We will discuss this story in more detail in chapter 7. For now, simply note the contrast between a plain, unimaginative "Christian" and a picturesque, fully imaged "nonbeliever." That contrast is by no means new to the church; there have been times when the church embraced the arts, when Christians drew pictures and wrote poems with the blessing of the church; and there have been times when both paintings and stories were cast out and scorned by the church.

This book is about stories and the church and the imagination. It is about the relationship between literature and theology, the relationship between contemporary stories and the way Christians talk about their faith. It will encourage modern Christians to read modern literature. Beyond all this, however, the book springs from a way of understanding a Christian's background.

The Christian's life and faith are shaped within a community that exists because of the great *story* of God's freeing and sustaining love.

The Bible tells that story; the church has repeated it, lived it, been nourished by it for centuries. We are a people who know how to read a story and how to tell one. We also know how to interpret a story, how to make sense of it. God's gift of imagination helps with the hearing, the telling, and the interpreting.

As a community born of a story, the church knows something about the value of narrative. As a community of interpretation, the church has the ability to understand, to explain, and to enjoy a narrative. We are the people of God living in the closing decades of the twentieth century, and we find ourselves armed with God's story in a world of both confusion and opportunity. In that world, contemporary literary artists—novelists, short-story writers, poets, playwrights—tell their stories about human existence: they not only entertain us, they sometimes bewilder us, sometimes help us understand ourselves and our period of history, sometimes uphold common human values. Because in the church we are storytellers ourselves, we listen also to those modern tales and use our own experiences within the community of faith for comprehending stories that, even though they seem foreign to us, will have some kinship with our own narratives. As we enter a dialogue of sorts with contemporary writers and readers, we learn something about their skills of interpretation, and we begin to apply those skills to the reading of their stories and to the study of our own narratives as well.

This book, then, is about the relationship between God's story and modern fiction. I intend to explore what the fields of literature and theology have to do with one another, what problems arise when dialogue occurs between them, and how those problems might be approached. I intend to suggest a theological framework for this task and to pursue the whole matter in a way that respects the uniqueness and value of both fields. I will review means of analyzing, discussing, and evaluating fiction, and I will study some particular modern stories as illustrations of how such examination might be undertaken. I intend to work this agenda out in a language not overly burdened with jargon—a language that will be accessible to people without special training in literary criticism or advanced theological discourse.

The book is also about stories and the church and the imagination. This is not, in other words, an attempt to argue all the issues that have arisen in discussions of literature and theology. A great deal has been written about that relationship (see the first note in chapter 1), and many of the questions get extremely complicated. I am not so much entering those debates as I am trying to make available to the general reader some critical tools and some theological resources for his or her study and reading. I do not mean to oversimplify the complex questions, but I also do not want to follow every issue into its every intricacy. This is more a book for pastors, college and seminary students, members of congregations, than it is a book for professional theologians and literary critics. My hope is that groups of Christians who are interested in modern literature will derive some help in reading, analyzing, and discussing contemporary stories and, in the process, that they will find renewed interest in God's story as their strength and their commission.

The material here comes to its present form as the result of many years of reading, pondering, and teaching, but specifically it took shape through the generous gift of a sabbatical leave. That leave was made possible by Aid Association for Lutherans and its Franklin Clark Fry Presidential Fellowship. I am more grateful for that award than I can adequately express; it has proven to be an overwhelming gift of time for reflection, study, and enjoyment. I also express appreciation to the Lutheran Theological Southern Seminary, its president, Mack C. Branham, and its Board of Trustees, for allowing me to have a year free from other responsibilities, and to the seminary's former president, Hugh George Anderson, for his encouragement and friendship over two decades. Especially I thank my colleagues Professors Scott H. Hendrix and Michael J. Root for reading parts of the manuscript and making valuable suggestions; remaining weaknesses are surely not their fault, but they did contribute to some of the strengths. A substantial sabbatical grant from the Lutheran Brotherhood Insurance Company made it possible for me to have needed books and supplies as well as secretarial assistance and to take trips for research and writing: I am grateful to them for their support. Not least, I thank Anne and Catherine and Mark for their love and patience.

St. Bartholomew, Apostle   C.F.
August 24, 1984

Part I

1

EXPLORING

God, the great imaginer, loves to tell stories. Human beings enjoy stories too, and they sometimes like to talk about God. Although telling stories and talking about God may seem to be two distinct activities, they often overlap. People hear stories in church, read stories in books, see stories on film.

The initial question, then, is how one can talk about the overlapping of God's stories and human stories and still be sensitive to the integrity of each. Put another way, this is an exploration of the relationship between literature and theology—an exploration that seeks to respect the independence of each field but that is also concerned with how the two fields might function and how they might affect life in the church. Numerous complications beset this sort of discussion, not the least being the difficulty of advocating one particular theological approach in a society where many people believe many different things and express their beliefs using so many different words and images. How does one settle on a particular theology without alienating all the people who hold contrary positions? How can one be so narrow as to advocate a single stance? Facing those questions I intend, in this chapter, to present a theological framework for this discussion and to argue, at the same time, that literature must be taken seriously in terms of having its own principles and territory.

Scholars who have written about the relationship between literature and theology have presented a variety of theological positions to support their own approaches. Some cite Paul Tillich, some Dietrich Bonhoeffer; others attempt to build only on Scripture and so claim superiority; still others work in more philosophical realms and structure their method on Aristotle or Heidegger or Whitehead. Some scholars inevitably try to come up with a new angle, arguing that positions A, B, and C have problems and presenting a new superior position D. The purpose here is not to dispute those positions: many of them have considerable merit. Perhaps not everyone will be interested in the intricacies of the arguments, though; for those who are, the bibliographical notes will list scholarly resources.[1] What I intend to do, instead, is step back from the academic arguments and try to work out a theological framework that has an integrity of its own and that respects the integrity of the literature. Many essays eventually wind up shortchanging one or the other: either the authors are so theologically oriented that they hardly listen to the literature at all, so busy are they finding biblical allusions and evidence of the storyteller's religious interests; or they are so concerned with the literature—its beauty, its form, its message—that they forget the theology altogether. Still a third possibility, of course, is that they argue for the integrity of the two fields; but before they are finished they have made it plain that theology is, after all, uppermost in their interest. They will say things like, "of course, we shouldn't use the term 'Christian literature,'" and by the end of the essay they get around to how they would define "Christian literature" if they were to use it.

Much can be said for letting a variety of approaches stand. Scholars of various persuasions—divergent understandings of Christianity as well as differing schools of literary criticism—can and should make their cases for relating or not relating stories with discussions about God. Agreement about a single method for understanding this relationship between literature and theology is not required; that would be boring even if it were possible. This book does not claim to have now found the one new approach that will solve all critical problems. Rather, I will assume that different interpretations, different critical approaches, and openness to surprising possibilities all contribute to the reader's enjoyment and benefit. The argument is for diversity.[2]

What follows, then, is a theological framework that can stand on its own as respectable theology. It is a framework that has, built in, a place for literature as an independent area with its own warrants and authenticities. To say that a theological framework has a "place" for literature may sound imperialistic, but I hope to show that the "place" is really substantial, not at all narrow. I intend to illustrate how these two fields might be understood as having some clear relationship without one dominating the other or ignoring the other or romanticizing the other. In later chapters, I will present some literary principles and provide some guidelines for responsible, thorough criticism, unencumbered by theological presuppositions. Here the concern is with the theology. This theological position, though it is not new, will provide a common ground for discussing literature and theology and for examining the connections between the church and imagination, between God's story and modern fiction.[3]

A THEOLOGICAL FRAMEWORK

The first thing to say is the most obvious: God made and makes everything that is. God has a fantastic imagination and can think up the most beautiful, the most unlikely, the most puzzling combinations: planets and black holes; moonlight over a lake; whales and shrimp; armadillos on a desert. God did not sit down one day and actually envision moonlight over a lake and decide that would be a nice touch for the creatures. Rather, God caused the lake to be and the moonlight to be, and the combination as it appears on a given romantic evening is one of God's bonuses. A million things have happened that way. God did not actually produce in their present states a silicon chip, a telescope, a squeeze play in baseball, or a poem that begins, "When I consider how my light is spent." Still, God made the raw materials, the language, the brains from which all this has come; God has given human beings the capacity to imagine and invent and enjoy. The psalmist said it: "The earth is the Lord's and the fullness thereof." That is first. God is creator of all that is. God is creator, preserver, housekeeper, caretaker, gardener, handmaid, sweeper, timekeeper, and with it all, ruler. Like a hen brooding over her chicks, God watches out for all this earth, all these humans, animals, planets, things. The earth is God's.

People have some trouble these days finding appropriate metaphors to talk about God. A metaphor is usually defined as a comparison of two unlike objects whereby the known object clarifies or provides a picture for the unknown object. "God is King" is a metaphor, and what we know about kings is supposed to tell us what we do not know about God. The problem is that when we talk about God we recognize that most human images have limitations. Some kings, after all, are tyrannical, some fathers drunken, some housekeepers sloppy, some managers impersonal, some friends disloyal; we are not likely to find one point of comparison that will satisfy us all. In the following pages, my use of metaphors for God will be guided by two simple principles: one, to avoid strictly masculine images; and two, to employ a variety of metaphors—recognizing their limits, but hoping that by changing the language from time to time we can resist the fixed comparison and allow the variety to fill out our sense of God's own breadth. So I will talk of God guiding, managing, caring (as caretaker and caregiver), and overseeing and ruling and loving and leading and watching—all in an effort to portray something of the scope of God's activity for us. These metaphors are still not perfect: some guides get lost, some overseers overlook details, some caretakers fall asleep behind the barn. But then, part of the point—when we make metaphors for God—is that God fulfills those human roles to their very best and will "neither slumber nor sleep."[4]

Most Christians, and even some non-Christians, have agreed about God's role as creator and ruler and preserver. Disagreement has come about just how God could manage it all or whether God even tried, apart from a few winks and nods from some distant throne. The Bible is clear, however, about how God managed, even though the story is complex and some of the impressions vary from one storyteller to the next. In the biblical narrative, God is not the distant one watching over the earth with indifference or wry amusement. Rather, God is busy making things happen, involved up to the ears in the ordinary activities of the people who walk this earth. God even walked it a few times, they say. In fact, those storytellers often present God as one of the major characters of a narrative: sometimes helping people out, sometimes calling them to account, always trying to convince them about God's own power and authority and love.

Still, the question may persist, despite the Bible's stories, as to how God can be said to be creator, preserver, and ruler today. Much of the evidence seems to point much more clearly to God's absence or to the loss of any God at all: millions of people are starving; the world's military powers seem bent on destroying this earth with an absurd stockpile of nuclear weapons; warfare and terrorism dot the globe; drugs ruin lives; personal relationships crumble; chemical and nuclear wastes, disease, decreasing resources threaten all the earth's inhabitants. The creator seems to have abandoned the creation; the preserver is letting things go to waste; the housekeeper is napping on the sofa; the ruler must have abdicated.

It takes some nerve to stand up in the face of all that is falling apart and talk about God as creator, preserver, and ruler. Those who profess such a faith need not be surprised if cynics laugh at them and the poor raise angry fists and the hungry fix them with empty stares. This is a difficult problem. One cannot affirm God's care of the earth without a confidence about who God is and a grounding in the biblical narrative. This is an issue, therefore, that will require further development later in the chapter; for the moment, I should like to begin with an assertion of faith that—all appearances to the contrary—God is creator, preserver, ruler.

Even if that statement is accepted, another problem arises. Just how does God handle it all? Of course, we can say that God is all-powerful, all-knowing, able to see and do and affect any and everything. That challenge to the imagination—God as computer programmer sitting at a mammoth keyboard and screen?—needs some attention and perhaps some correction. Can we talk about God as all-powerful and at the same time say that God does not just sit around all day punching in commands or pulling switches? That seems to be the way many people think about God—as though God were directly responsible for every-thing that happens on this earth, as though God ordered each auto-mobile accident, each cancerous growth, each devastating storm (or if God did not order them, at least God saw them developing and refused to lift a finger to prevent them). In this view of God's way of ruling, God also decided in favor of one football team when they go at one another on a field, and God decides in favor of one nation when they go at one another on the battleground. God determines the election of each city official, each governor and president, each bishop and pastor.

Can we say that God creates, preserves, and rules without also saying that God pulls every switch to make every single thing on earth happen as it does? We can, primarily because the Bible certainly does not show God operating with such control. In biblical stories, time and time again, people wonder where God can be and have to tackle their problems with their own best wisdom or muddle through with their own limited judgment. True, God acts in their history: deliv-erance from the Egyptians, settlement in a fertile land, establishment of a nation under a mighty king. I suspect though that they, like us, only knew of God's immediate firsthand role in their lives by looking backward. Only when they had come to the end of a journey did they see that God had been guiding them; only when they sat down to tell the story did they realize it was really God's story and not just their own.

The question remains: How does God do it? It isn't a matter of magically pulling rabbits from hats, waving wands. Nor is it a matter of scientific capability: punching a keyboard and keeping a meticulous filing system. The biblical record suggests that God has two basic ways of taking care of things, and numerous teachers of the church down through the years have developed and argued for these two basic patterns of God's caretaking. For one thing, God trusts the creation, knows the product, and lets it work. God guides through the creation, letting the patterns there take care of themselves, letting the creatures use their brains and muscles to handle, control, guide, help or harm, think, write, love, and hate.

God knows the creation well enough, however, to know its limitations and its inclination to do things its own way, so God has another way of guiding. This second way is even more foolhardy than the first. God loves; God forgives; God provides ways for human beings to know that they are valuable, cared for, and that the world is not finally in their hands but in God's. God runs mighty risks with these ways of taking care of us all. Pulling strings and punching a keyboard would, no doubt, be more efficient and more effective—at least if measured by human standards of judgment. God, however, prefers a different pattern, so God creates and God loves. That is the heart of the divine caretaking plan.

What is essential for this discussion is that one God is both creator and lover. It is impossible to separate these two dimensions: the creator loves, the lover creates. Outrageous as it may seem, the same God who made this earth and watches over it is the very God who loves it to death. That seems outrageous because, as was noted above, the evidence sometimes contradicts such a judgment, and the people of the earth get the impression that the God who made it all went away and forgot about what had been made. It seems outrageous too that anyone could love the things of this earth literally to death. Human beings are terribly selective in their love; one can imagine loving a few people enough to die for them, but loving *all* people that much? Not likely. Because we can discriminate in our loving, because we can destroy the things and the people we dislike, we assume God might work the same way. But then, we do not know God, the one God who both keeps house and loves each nook and cranny, who makes all people and loves them all whatever their own peculiar rebellions and atrocities. To make such an outrageous claim is to speak as one who believes and trusts God. If you do not know deeply and intimately who God is or what God does, of course, you cannot understand how God can be creator or lover, much less both rolled up into one. I will have to say more about how we come to such a statement of trust, but for now, the point is that the God who has two ways of guiding, the God who is both preserver and forgiver, is nonetheless one God. God's own intentions are always interacting between the two ways of caretaking. The nurturer of believers watches over all the creation; the caretaker of the universe calls each creature "my beloved."

In Christian thought, this basic design has often been spoken of as the twofold rule of God or—to use technical terms—the distinction of the two kingdoms. Some people argue that this distinction should be forever abandoned because it has so many inadequacies. They point out that it has been abused and misunderstood; they blame everything from American blue laws to the holocaust of the 1930s and 1940s on just this way of understanding God's care of the world. The problem, of course, is that to a large degree those critics of the distinction are right. No matter how neatly anyone—even an Augustine or a Luther—might work out the idea, the argument inevitably seems to mean something quite different when it hits the streets. So, people have said, "Yes, God rules in two ways: with the law and reason in society and its institutions, and with love and faith in the church and its ministries. Therefore [and here comes the problem], the church and society must forever stand apart from one another and have nothing to do with one another: the church to take care of our spiritual lives [whatever that means] and the state and society to take care of our temporal needs [whatever that means]." Such an understanding has allowed the church to look the other way when injustices were going on in the society, as though whether or not people had enough food to eat or useful work to perform were matters of total indifference to a person's "spiritual" well-being. This and a host of other problems— even the term "kingdom" may seem too triumphalist and colonialist for use in the twentieth century—render the whole approach useless today, argue its critics.

So why drag it out and try to rescue it? One reason is that the problems associated with this distinction do not necessarily follow from the idea itself. One can talk, therefore, about a twofold rule of God if one is careful to state the case precisely and guard against misinterpretations, if one acknowledges the problems and avoids the confusing terminology. Another reason for talking about the two ways God takes care of us and this earth lies in the conviction that such an approach can help us understand how two areas such as literature and theology, which seem on the face of it to be so totally different and unrelated, can exist in healthy tension. The twofold pattern helps me clarify their relationship without letting them blend into one another and without leaving one superior to the other, thereby controlling the functions of the other. This is no startling new interpretation, nor is it merely the revival of an old and treasured, but abused, teaching. It is, though, an approach that can be helpful so long as we admit its difficulties and proceed cautiously.

GOD AS CREATOR AND PRESERVER

Having given the basic structure and acknowledged some of the problems of this theological framework, I can now examine in more detail, first, God's way of guiding as creator, preserver, ruler. Here, God guides by letting the creation work. God provides the resources and grants freedom, and things begin to happen. And such things they are! People love one another and make more people; someone invents hopscotch and baseball and Monopoly and a Rubik's Cube; others invent wheels and flying machines and computers. Some of the things we have come up with seem to be so standard, so obviously important and necessary to our well-being, that we are inclined to say God must have had them in mind all along. They must have been a part of that original divine imagination. We have governments, for example, that for all their variety of form and for all their abuses and weaknesses are vital to our continued lives together on this planet. Whether God wanted us to organize as capitalists or socialists, Republicans or Democrats, we cannot really determine—although people will make their own case, assuring themselves that God is on their side. What is clear is that God wants us to live in some kind of order and peace and harmony. Just as there must be governments, so it seems there must be some kind of family life, some form of economics, and some form of human creative expression that we might call the arts. We have no guidebook that says human beings have to live in a democratic, capitalistic society, married to only one person, producing only 2.2 children in a lifetime, having only drawings by Norman Rockwell on their walls, and listening only to golden oldies on the radio. God may be happy when we do some of these things, terribly disappointed by others. The point is that God does not prescribe these things; instead, God takes the awesome risk of letting us find our own way, organize and amuse and feed and defend ourselves as we will.

God is not the kind of god, of course, who has abdicated anything by this policy of caretaking. God keeps the whole system intact, watches, applauds, weeps, nudges, oversees, prods. Consider the biblical tales where God keeps turning up, raising up heroes and heroines, time after time, just when it seemed as though no one were minding the store. So the people of Israel are in desperate slavery under cruel taskmasters, and Moses is off in the wilderness tending to somebody else's sheep, and God comes along, in flames, to pack off an unwilling and unlikely deliverer and initiate a pattern of divine rescue that is to tell people forever about the kind of god God really is. By entrusting the submanagement of the earth to human beings—by subcontracting in a sense—God knows what is going on, knows the risks and the great potential, and everything that happens falls under the watchful, preserving, and ruling eye. And still God leads, abdicating nothing.

One small part of God's great everything is literature. This is not to diminish literature by any means but to give it its place in the created order. One of God's gifts is that people should be able to imagine and think and write out their imaginings and thoughts in beautiful and engaging patterns; that they should be able to remember and tell stories and try to get at elusive truths; that they should attempt to understand themselves and pass on to their children what they have counted most important about life. Whether we think of literature in its broadest sense as anything that is written (essays, treatises, histories) or use the term more narrowly to refer to imaginative works (fiction, drama, poetry), it all comes under God's guidance as creator, preserver, ruler, inasmuch as God endows the human mind with the capacity for imagination and language and reason. This gift is available to all of humanity whether or not a person believes there is a God who is creator of the earth, who preserves and rules it. Whether or not a person acknowledges in any way who God is, still, God's gifts are there. Most people can think and imagine—some more effectively, more creatively than others—and most can express their thoughts and images in some way, by making signs or telling stories or writing down what they have thought and imagined.

Trusting that the gifts come from God does not necessarily make a person a better thinker, imaginer, or writer; nor does skill in these arts suggest that a person, regardless of opinions, is somehow closer to God. God does not teach these skills or bestow them on favorites. Rather, the ability to think and imagine and write well is a skill that, we might say, comes to human beings naturally, just as does the ability to build a house or sew a dress or sail a boat or bake a cake. Those skills come naturally, though not, of course, equally: some people seem to have a natural ability to write a poem but could never bake a cake anyone would want to eat; others can sail beautifully but do battle with words the way still others might battle wind currents. Being able to do any one of these things will not necessarily make us healthier people, nor will it guarantee us happiness and peace. We may find certain satisfactions in our gifts and talents, but we may also experience frustrations, disappointments, and sorrows through them. These gifts may also bring us responsibilities and tensions, and they may lead us into new territory, into new and perhaps painful knowledge of our world and ourselves. They may even set us on a path toward perfection as we aspire to an absolute form, to combining words in just the right patterns of beauty and sense. We are not likely to find that because we can write a sonnet or lay bricks we are able to hold our tempers and be always kind and loving. So literature—neither the writing of it nor the reading of it—does not offer us lasting wholeness; that is, literature does not have, as its specific assignment, the unmistakable, explicit announcement of God's forgiving, sustaining love. It does offer benefits in a more commonplace dimension of our existence. Its significance rests not in its proclamation of the gospel but in its address to all people in terms of fundamental issues of life. To say that literature's benefits are commonplace is not to call them unimportant but is rather to recognize their widespread and lasting human value.

The Benefits of Literature

The true personal benefits of literature cannot be cataloged by anyone except the individual reader. But we do not read for the benefits alone, nor are we always conscious of the dividends reading may provide: few people open a novel or go to a movie thinking in advance how they will be rewarded for their reading or viewing. The point here is simply that some benefits do come to the reader, and there is advantage in recognizing what those benefits might be.

Literature can, for example, entertain us. Sometimes that is all we want from it: a few hours of escape from the monotony of our own lives, some adventure we will never have in person. When we "curl up with a good book" or take an evening off for the movies (much of what we say about literature applies to film as well, of course) we want to be amused, to be transfixed, and we surely don't want anyone asking us perplexing moral or philosophical questions about what we have read or seen. In literature that we approach for entertainment, there may well be significant moral or philosophical questions, but we may choose not to think about them because thinking about them would destroy the very purpose we had for reading the book in the first place—that is, escape from perplexing questions of life. This is not to pass any negative judgment on reading for entertainment. Enjoyment is part of God's creation too. For those who cannot take an ocean cruise to evade boredom, a compelling story borrowed from the public library is a welcome substitute and an adequate vehicle for refreshment.

We may enjoy literature, of course, not only for dramatic stories but also for the beauty of its language, and that is another dimension of its entertainment value. People who especially like words may derive great satisfaction from the way a writer can form sentences and paragraphs, combine and play with meanings and sounds, make mere letters on a page describe with accuracy and forcefulness some personal characteristic, natural scene, or historic event. A work of literature need not match someone's definition of beauty in order to merit attention. For one thing, who is to decide what is meant by beauty, since a reader's own taste enters into such a judgment? For another, beauty may be deceptive, may even be false. A writer may describe in flowing phrases and delightful words some piece of reality—say, plantation life in the old South—and at the same time miss, or cause the reader to miss, alternate views of that reality, the inevitable pain and heartache and delusion of that system. Beauty is ambiguous. Dostoyevsky defined beauty as the battleground "where God and the Devil contend with one another" for human hearts.[5] As we appreciate the importance of beauty in a work of literature, we do so with some caution: still, beauty will remain one of the reasons we enjoy a novel or a poem or a play. Reading for entertainment—for beautiful language or for the pleasure of escape—is enough on occasion. Sometimes, however, we might derive even more from a good book.

A second benefit from literature is that it can help us understand our world, our culture, our own society and times. By knowing our world and culture we may be better prepared to tell our own stories of God's love to our contemporaries;[6] and we may live out our lives more purposefully, with perspective and health. The literary artist is not usually a sociologist or a historian; yet he or she has matured in a particular place and time. As a keen observer of the surroundings and people, as a careful analyst of the events and institutions of the social order, this artist may be able to lead us to new understandings of our own time and place. We will not always agree with another person's observations and analyses, of course, but questions will have been raised that we will no longer be able to ignore, and perhaps our own viewpoint will begin to change. At the very least it will be enlarged by our having entered—even tentatively—the perspective of another person. For this discussion, our starting point has been that the world is ultimately God's: whether or not the artist shares our sense of God's proprietorship over the earth, we remain co-inhabitants of that earth; our observations are mutually enriching. If we want to expand our vision of God's world, we will listen to the voices of those who see it from a different angle. As I read Flannery O'Connor's stories of fundamentalist Christians or displaced intellectuals, I find I have a new sensitivity toward people I otherwise might have dismissed too easily.[7] As I read Alice Walker's stories of black women in the South, I enter a world otherwise closed to me. I do so inadequately, since I am so far removed from that world in my daily experience, but I am able to catch a glimpse of the richness and pain of God's earth more fully for having made the entrance.[8]

A third benefit, related to the second but at yet another level, is that literature can help us understand ourselves more completely. A part of self-understanding comes from knowing more about the environment in which we have lived and knowing more about the other people with whom, in some degree, we have worked and played. We can, of course, read psychology or go through therapy or reflect carefully on our experiences and so come to know more about ourselves; but, to the degree that a sensitive writer portrays a character with accuracy or makes a character in a story a genuine human being, we may well find that we have personality features in common with that character. As that character's story unfolds and we identify with him or her, we begin to see our own lives worked out—to a limited degree, to be sure—on the page in front of us. As we come to understand the character, we may come to understand ourselves just a little better. Why does Nancy Finch in Doris Betts's *Heading West* seem to fall in with her kidnapper's plan and run from her home and family?[9] To what degree am I like Nancy Finch? Would I react as she does? If I understand her reaction, might I not also understand my own? If she finds resolution and makes a new start, might not I also? For us to get much help toward self-knowledge, we will have to consider such questions realistically and move from the world of fiction to our own situations; a good story may just make that opportunity possible.

The fourth benefit is much more difficult to discuss with precision. Literature can also present values and ideals that are clarifying or helpful to us. The words "values" and "ideals" provide the broadest dimension of what is intended in this category: much will be included here, and some things will be excluded. For example, a work of literature may well manage to convince us that the vision of our own region of the country is limited and shortsighted; a poem or a story may lead us to a broader sense of the whole human community and thereby call into question some of the values and ideals we have theretofore thought essential. The value "love of one's own home territory"—be that a county or a country—is now placed beside another value, "love of the whole earth." The second may replace the first, or they may coexist for a while, or despite the persuasion of the piece of literature, we may conclude that our first value is really the more essential and is in fact threatened by the second. Should this last be our conclusion, the literature would not have seemed to make any change in our opinion, but it would at least have presented a challenge to our own values and so begun a process of thought that will work itself out sometime in the future.

Another way literature might present such values would be to remind us of ideas that have been held to be important by some people in times past. The strength of such a reminder will depend to some extent on our familiarity with those earlier values. If we have read none of the literature of classical Greece, references to the standards of Ulysses may pass us by without much influence, and if we have forgotten what we knew of Shakespeare, an allusion to his ideas will escape us. By the same token, if we know the Bible and find a reference, for example, to Abraham's faith, we are immediately carried beyond the work of literature itself to another story from another time, and as we put the two together and add them to our own experience, we gain some deeper sense of the meaning of faith. The writer, in such an instance, has selected the allusion without knowing whether or not all—or any—of her readers will be able to make a connection, though she hopes they can because that will enrich their reading. The point here has nothing to do with the writer's own acceptance of the ideal that the allusion evokes (for a discussion of how allusions work see chapter 3); the point is simply that literature can call forth such values, and we can respond to them as we are able to make the necessary connections.

Please notice that I am not calling these "religious" values. Many scholars in the field of literature and theology praise literature specifically because of its capacity for presenting religious values and themes. Clearly, some literature does present values that might be identified as "religious"; that term requires definition, however, and it would be next to impossible to get even a few people to agree on a suitable definition. For some, "religious literature" would have to deal especially with a person's relationship with God (such as poems by the seventeenth-century metaphysical poets—Donne or Herbert, for example). For others, literature is religious if it awakens in the reader a sense of wonder or of the Other (here a poem by Emerson or a story by Hawthorne would qualify). Still other critics might want the literature to convey unambiguously the gospel if it is to be considered religious (as do tales of C. S. Lewis). Now, it is fine to call all those works religious, but it is not very helpful to do so. The term simply doesn't mean the same thing to everyone, and to use it at this point clouds the issue. It is enough to say that literature presents values: human values, values that people have recognized to be important in times past and that seem to have continued influence today.

The Place of Literature in the Creation

More can no doubt be said about the benefits of literature. Each reader may be able to think of many other ways literature has been of special help to him or her. Literature also presents problems, however: just as it may inspire, it may also depress; just as it may show human nobility, it may also illustrate all too plainly human depravity. It may amuse readers, or it may bore them. It may tell more than anyone wants to know about how some people live, and so it may be a negative influence. If we are to talk responsibly about a relationship between literature and theology, we have to face this side of the matter as well as the other. Having some sense of literature's place in the whole scheme of things helps us to deal with its possible bad influences as well as with its general points of contact with theology.

That place in the scheme of things is a place within God's creative, preserving, ruling way of caring for this earth and its people. Literature derives its authenticity and its creativity and its imaginative power from God, the original, creative imaginer; it comes from God as surely as do human bodies and modern technology and sports and gardening. People may not want to give God any credit, but as creator, preserver, ruler, God initiates and watches over and nudges both those who know who God is and those who don't, both nonbelievers and believers. As a part of God's creation, literature functions with ordinary human reason and imagination—gifts available to all God's creatures—and in that function it has potential for helping everyone to keep things straight on this earth. Literature may assist in God's preserving, housekeeping tasks by helping people understand the whole human community, by reminding them of social responsibility, by awakening them to the requirements of justice. In literature, in other words, God preserves society through the writer, just as in the political arena God rules society through legislators. Again, the writer may no more give God a nod of allegiance than the politician might; both might be indignant at the mere suggestion that God had anything to do with their work (though politicians have been known to use God when they felt a little name-dropping might get a few votes). For all that, God continues to create, preserve, and rule, and literature is one of the means.

This position for literature supports its own independence and integrity as a distinct field of activity. When we consider literature as a part of God's creative, preserving, ruling strategy, we need to expect that literature should be something more than it is. We need not expect literature to tell us directly about God or present the gospel or preach or convert. When it falls short of our highest expectations as a means of presenting values, we know that it must fail at that task, since it is a limited form, produced by human beings who, while they are God's creatures, do not always acknowledge God's rule—and, indeed, often deny it and rebel against it. The theologian, then, need not think that literature by itself will do the theologian's job and the Christian need not think that literature, to be any good, must preach the gospel and effect conversions. None of that is literature's work. Literature has its own noble task.

Because we may be inclined to credit literature with more than it can possibly bear and turn it into a surrogate priest, perhaps an analogy will clarify its role. Baseball belongs to the area of creation just as does literature, and it exists independently from theology. While the independence and integrity of baseball may seem obvious, it might well be possible for some ardent baseball fan to make a case for baseball as one of God's agents for bringing health and wholeness to people. One might talk, for example, about the symmetry of the game, the beauty of the human form stretching for a pitch or leaping for a fly ball, the ultimate fairness of the game (every batter with three strikes, each team with twenty-seven outs), the authority and impartiality of the umpire. One might say—some have—there is something almost mythical about the game, something religious, perhaps even something redemptive. In the early spring of 1983, about sixty Chicago businessmen completed a week in Arizona (at something over two thousand dollars apiece) practicing with and then playing a game against the 1969 Chicago Cubs; these nonprofessional sportsmen talked about a week of renewal and fulfillment and joy.[10] We need not doubt the value of their experience: the ecstasy of playing that game and the sense of community with the other players are both characteristics associated with religious experience. However much one might like the sport, however, baseball is not God's primary way of assuring us love and acceptance; only the gospel can do that finally. But baseball may well be one of God's best imaginings, a part of creation that is meant to be enjoyed, one avenue to some measure of health and happiness for some people. To try to turn baseball into God's way of forgiving and making people ultimately whole is to distort the created order and to rob the game of its own unique role. Literature also deserves its own place, and an honored place it is.

Literature can entertain us, can help us understand our world and ourselves, and can present values to us. Indeed, as it does these things, literature fulfills its place in God's creating and preserving plan. This honored role, however, has one hidden quality: somehow without being conscious of what it is doing, literature prepares us for hearing specifically in another time and place about the fullness of God. The author will not likely realize this is happening, nor will the reader; this is a hidden quality. Literature will not proclaim God's best news, but it may prime us to hear that news.

Earlier, when I described God's two ways of ruling and caring, I insisted that God is, after all, one God, preserver and lover. God's own intentions are always interacting between the two ways of caretaking. The divine lover preserves the creation and prepares the ground whereon we might come to know both preservation and love. We could say that God does this in every dimension of the creating and preserving plan—in the natural world, in baseball, in silicon chips, in literature—and always God's intentions remain hidden. Only as we hear the good news explicitly, through Word and Sacrament, do we begin to understand that we have been prepared in ways beyond our reckoning, that we have been primed by many other experiences in our lives for this moment of special joy. Hidden qualities cannot bear much description. To make this claim for literature is not to contradict what has gone before, nor is it to claim too much; it is simply to recall, in another way, that the God who preserves is also God who loves, that the plans of caregiving are integrated; that God is always getting us ready for the surprise of love; that God prepares the way through our wildernesses.[11]

GOD AS GIVER OF WHOLENESS

God has to worry about watching over everybody and everything, so God is housekeeper and preserver. God also has to worry about taking care of Christian believers, and that is quite an operation. God's rule over Christian believers has to do with the things God does to make sure we hear the good news of God's love, to nourish us in our confidence about who God is, to bind us in a community of believers who will both love us and need our love. Here God is a deliverer releasing the prisoners, a mother teaching and feeding her children, a doctor healing human brokenness, a lover yearning for the beloved. Now we are talking about the faith and trust of the believer. What God guides under this rule are the health and wholeness of the creatures—what we have always called "salvation" and "redemption" in the language of the church; but this health and wholeness are not simply some qualities to be attained or granted in a distant future, some time and place after our lives on earth. God promises the gift of health and wholeness as we live our days on earth; Jesus announced that God's rule has already begun. Nor is this gift a matter of physical or psychological well-being: it may include "good health" in the more traditional sense of the phrase, but it also may not. Salvation, God's gift of health and wholeness, has more to do with a confidence within the believer, a sense of having some things together, a sense of understanding a mystery, a way of living comfortably without having loose ends tied up, a way of living "despite" all that is wrong and threatening and unsettling. God's gift already belongs to the believer in spite of signs to the contrary; God's rule has begun.

Just as God preserves the lives of all people through the governments of the earth and their representatives, so God rules the lives of believers through the church and its ministers, through the Word and Sacraments. God's message to us—God's Word—is, under this form of caretaking, much more direct and explicit. The message is accompanied by a promise and is repeated within a special community of people who have trusted the promise and seen it fulfilled over and over again. For this assurance of who God is and how God loves, we cannot depend on our own instincts; as was noted above, our instincts lead us to think God is no longer around. For this assurance, we are dependent on God taking some special steps to break through to us in what might be considered "unnatural" ways. Within the community of believers, Christians can talk about the ways they are shown who God is and how God loves; but when they do so outside the community, other people may well wag their tongues and level charges that the Christians are no longer being very reasonable. And they aren't. God has unveiled a plan.

The heart of this plan of caretaking becomes clear in the story in Jesus of Nazareth. When God wanted to let people know the divine intention that they live in health and wholeness, God enacted a story that would demonstrate who God is and how God loves, a story that could then be retold and re-presented by the community of believers to sustain assurance of the message. In Jesus, God unveils the plan. Through the life and teachings, the death and new life of Jesus, God lets us know that we are each loved and honored by the very God of all that is. When we feel guilty about our weaknesses and mistakes and distrust, God tells us we are accepted just as we are; when we feel alone and empty, God speaks the promise, "I am with you always." It is precisely through Jesus that we know about God's presence and acceptance of us, for Jesus was so like what God had promised, and some people who saw him and heard him knew that he must be God, as outrageous a claim as that might be. This is the church's confession: Jesus is the one promised by God from the oldest times to set people free and to love without qualification.

This is not, however, simply an announcement broadcast over a loudspeaker, "God is love; everything's going to be OK. As you were." This is rather a staggering intervention, God breaking into human history at a particular place and time, becoming a human being, knowing human pain and suffering, dying and despairing ("Why have you forsaken me?"), and—incredible as it may seem— passing beyond those limitations to new and triumphant life again. Such a dramatic action reaches to the very core of our existence.

But it isn't just that God had to use a flannelgraph or put on a puppet show to get folks finally to catch on. God had been loving and forgiving for years and had put on some impressive demonstrations; the people of Israel did not forget or misunderstand the exodus, God leading them out of slavery and oppression; they even sang about and told the stories of God's steadfast and faithful love. The problem was, and still is, that we refuse to believe it all; we turn our backs, scoff at love, rebel against the ruler, scorn the caregiver. In Jesus, God some- how breaks through that deep rebellion and sets us free and turns us around and calls us beloved. There is no more "as you were" but new life. So God acts in history for us and works in our lives to heal a relationship we insist on breaking and to build a trust in that astound- ing love.

To know the meaning and the joy of that promise, we live in the church, the community of believers, as those who trust God's love; and we hear the story again and again. We walk through it each year as we worship from Advent through Pentecost. We recall the ex- pressions of God's promise to Abraham and Sarah, to Miriam and Moses, to Deborah and Samson and David; we hear the prophets announce the time that God will rule; we join the affirmation of the early church that Jesus is one with the God of creation and deliverance and that this very God is busy among us now making us a special people who know peace and wholeness and love and joy. Armed with this story we see ourselves—as individuals and as a community—as God's agents, God's own people called to "declare the wonderful deeds of the One who called us out of darkness into marvelous light" (1 Peter 2:9, RSV revised).

How can all this be? In any given church, there are people quite active in that community who lie and hate and are jealous and vicious. The church often ignores God's inclusive love and rule and behaves as though it ruled and could choose its own boundaries of love. We still feel bitterness and despair, still lose our tempers and our bearings, still want to run our own lives on our own terms. How can it be that God calls us a holy, special people?

There is the mystery! There is the joy! There is God's most amazing good news! God looks at us and sees Jesus; God looks at our indifference and sees Jesus' commitment; God looks at our longing for comfort and sees Jesus' cross; God looks at our fear of death and sees the stone rolled back and Jesus out talking about a whole new world. God looks at our disobedience, our distrust, our sin; and God sees the obedience and trust and perfection of Jesus. That is the astounding message God has for us! That is gospel! As we trust that promise, we know wholeness and health here and now. As we read the accounts of God's dealings with people in the past, we see that they came to understand and know God's Word to be true. So we live not by idle words but by the assurance that the promise has been fulfilled for countless millions of believers down through the years. We stand in that train, and we live and work in that community today where the story is told, the presence experienced, and the joy believed.

God's story has not yet come to an ending, of course. When you read a suspenseful novel, you may feel you're cheating if you turn to the last page and discover how it all comes out; doing so might deprive you of the pleasure of wondering and anticipating and being surprised. Another of the wonders of God's story is that we know the ending while we live through the middle of it, and still we move along in excitement. In the cross and resurrection of Jesus, God has already described the ending. Because God acted decisively in history, we know the story will conclude with victory, with judgment and power and life and triumph. We are not robbed of the suspense, however. How can this world with its apparent chaos and its cycles of violence and destruction really be under God's care? How can I, with my difficulty in hearing God's Word and my consistent resistance to it, be one who is really turned around? How can the church bear God's story along into so uncertain a future?

God promises to remain in control, to continue to guide and protect and preserve and love and create. God promises to bear us—church and world—into a future that is God's own, defined, described, controlled by God's love and energy and power. Not only have we not been abandoned, we will not be. So we make our way through life, hearing God's story as we travel, being given renewed confidence as we move along; being given assurance that God leads the way, accepts us, transforms us, urges us and encourages us to be the people of the caregiver, to take care of one another and of God's world, to move toward God's ending, God's triumphant beginning.

THE TENSION IN THE FRAMEWORK

In those two ways, God watches over the earth: as creator, preserver, and ruler, God cares for everyone and everything; as lover, healer, and forgiving presence, God cares for believers. And God is One. A major problem with this method of talking about what God does should be apparent by now: it splits up life and reality much too neatly. The problem is that you cannot talk about two things at once without taking them one at a time. When the church has in the past talked of God's two ways of ruling, we have made it seem as though they were two mutually exclusive, independent operations. We have not stressed sufficiently that the one God rules everything, that both ways of guiding are the strategy of the same God. Perhaps we have not said clearly enough that the believer lives always under both plans. That is, of course, what makes the whole thing so tricky and what needs some further discussion.

Each believer always lives both in the church and in the society. While that ought to be obvious, it has been forgotten or conveniently ignored. We forget it or ignore it when we think that we are, by virtue of our own sterling behavior, the very model of what everyone in society should become and so try to impose our standards on everyone else, including those who do not know and trust God's love. Under this scenario, the church sets itself up over the rest of society and tries to rule God's roost and wants to pass laws making everyone follow its prescriptions. Whenever this has happened, there has been a surplus of self-righteousness and, also, of pain for others of God's creatures who didn't quite measure up to the imposed standards. (This was the case at some times under medieval Catholicism and New England Puritanism, and it will be the case whenever some moral majority tries to rule all of society.) God takes care of both church and society under two plans, and believers live in both at once.

We might forget this also when we dismiss the church as irrelevant and out-of-touch, when we assume that society itself is more than adequate to take care of its own needs and to do all the ruling and preserving that people require. Under this scenario, we forget that God rules the social order, and we try to make it totally independent. Here we might think ourselves to be God and deny any standards but those that spring from human wisdom and reason. We have called this attitude "secularism," and it threatens because it ignores God. God rules both church and society, and believers live in both at once.

We forget this when we insist that church and society are really totally different entities and that the one has nothing to do with the other. We have a strict separation of church and state, and we follow one pattern of life on Sunday and another Monday through Saturday. We dissociate the life of faith from the life of reason and thereby tear asunder God's way of caregiving.

When we try to talk about a genuine relationship of church and society, both under God's rule, we find ourselves caught in an apparent contradiction. We seem to be wanting to have things both ways: both unity and difference, both church-and-society and church-separate-from-society. But there are reasons for wanting it both ways. We insist on the *difference* between God's two ways of guiding in order to avoid clericalism or triumphalism, that is, the rule of the church over the social order; and we insist on the *unity* of God's two ways of guiding in order to avoid secularism, that is, the rule of the state and society over the church in such a way that the church is unable to carry out its function of proclaiming the gospel, and in such a way that state and society make their own rules and call all the shots. There is a tension here, to be sure, and we are trying to walk a tightrope when we want to have it both ways. Despite the dangers, I am convinced there are advantages to at least attempting to accept the tension.[12]

One advantage is that we can perhaps understand ourselves a little better and get some perspective on the complicated tasks of our lives. We are not simply believers, trying to be obedient to God, enduring our daily lives as mere way stations on our journey to heaven. We are not simply churchgoers with folded hands and bowed heads, indifferent to the pains and injustices of our own lives and the lives of those around us. Some Christians may pretend that is the way their lives run, and many of us may long for the kind of patience and devotion such an image seems to suggest. For most of us, however, life is not that way: we have to earn a living and live in a society, and those demands put us in the position of making decisions and working with people who are not believers. We find that, while God may accept us as we are, other people often do not. Yet we know also that we are not simply citizens of the society, trying to make our way through the complicated issues of our times and relying only on our own good sense and the wisdom of other humans; we are not just voters and workers and players and readers, living by the clock for the moment. Rather, we live under both of God's caretaking plans at once, which means we understand that our lives are not broken into two different compartments but that what we do in society under God's rule is inevitably related to what we do in the church under God's rule. We need expect neither perfection in society nor absolute authority over all of life in the church. We seek those measures of justice that are most possible in the broader human community, and we trust God's love in the community of faith.

Another advantage of living with this tension is that we recognize the limitations of our lives in the social order. We do not expect the state to provide perfect peace and happiness, nor do we expect everyone to acknowledge God's rule. We ask neither the government nor literature nor sports to proclaim the gospel, and so we are not left in despair when they settle for what seems reasonable to most people rather than what seems most loving to a few. We know that civil laws will be broken, and we work within that order for responsible officials and responsible legislation and responsible punishments under the law. We do not expect too much; and we refuse to settle for too little.

Under the tension of living in both church and society at once, we also know of self-righteousness and forgiveness. Traditionally, the church has said that we are saints and sinners at the same time. While that may sound contradictory or impossible, if we think about our experience a little, we begin to find this a helpful tension. We know that in the decisions we must make in the public arena we most often find ourselves trapped between two poor choices: we must decide between two candidates, both of whom are less than we want for the office. We may even feel that we would be disobedient to God to vote for either one. But we know something about both sin and forgiveness, so we grit our teeth, vote for the one who seems the lesser of the two evils, and say our prayers for forgiveness. Over and over again, on issues of abortion, nuclear disarmament, capital punishment, environmental protection, we find ourselves confronted with immensely complex decisions. Not to decide would be an act of despair. To insist on one perfect and "Christian" response would be both hopeless strategy and self-righteous deception. So we sin boldly and believe confidently that God is indeed ruler and preserver and has a hand in the affairs of the social order and that, at the same time, God is forgiver and lover who both understands and loves in spite of our weaknesses and rebellions.[13]

Christians are, then, realists. We are willing to work within the corrupt and limited orders of society without expecting perfection; and we are content to live out our lives of faith in the church, confident of God's forgiveness. Neither idealists wanting only the most beneficial solution, nor fatalists thrown into inaction, we go to church, hear God's Word, say our prayers, talk together about the problems and decisions of our lives, and then go boldly about our daily business risking error and committing sin, knowing that we will commit it but preferring that to nothing. We study the context of a decision and make the best judgments we can; when we fail miserably in our strategy, we go back to the drawing board and try again. Free from the law by God's love, we uphold the law for the common good. Prodded by God's Word, we plead for the hungry and unemployed in the courts and legislative halls. We work as prophets denouncing injustice wherever it appears, and we call the church to enter that struggle by asking church members to be faithful in their civic responsibility. Luther provided some guidance for us in trying to figure when and how we enter that struggle:

> In what concerns you and yours, you govern yourself by the gospel and suffer injustices toward yourself as a true Christian; in what concerns the person or property of others, you govern yourself according to love and tolerate no injustice toward your neighbor.[14]

As citizens in society, we give our time and money to help the poor and needy; we are servants of the human community. We enlist others— nonbelievers as well—to serve their neighbors. We are realists working through tough decisions under God the creator, preserver, ruler and trusting confidently in God the present forgiver.

THE MEANING OF THE FRAMEWORK FOR LITERATURE

When we turn back to consider the effect of all this on the area of literature, we realize that there too we find not simplicity but complexity. I made the case for literature as an independent field under God's creating and preserving care of the earth. That sounds simple enough. What happens, though, when a Christian writes a poem? Will that poem be under the rule of love or under the rule of reason? Should the poem try to proclaim the gospel or celebrate the creation?

It ought to be clear that the Christian cannot stop being a Christian while the poem is being written and then pick up faith again away from pen and paper. He or she will be both believer and poet at the same time. That doesn't mean that the poem will have to proclaim the gospel, though it might; nor does it mean that the poet should try to remain neutral toward the gospel, though in a particular poem he or she might want to do just that. What it does mean is that we won't expect literature to preach the gospel, since that is not its function, and we won't judge literature on the basis of the gospel but on the basis of the standards within its own territory. Insofar as we are confident of God's love for us, we do not need literature to tell us that—nor, for that matter, do we need the sermon. But insofar as we are inclined to rebel against God's love and seek our own way in the world, we do need the sermon to proclaim the good news, and we can be grateful for any help literature might give us in understanding ourselves, our world, and human values.

This approach to God's two ways of caretaking, for all its deficiencies, at least helps us to place literature as an independent field under God's plan for the preservation of the earth. To talk about literature as an independent area does not mean that it is totally isolated from all other areas of life, or that it has nothing whatsoever to do with theology or with the experience of believers. It does mean that, in its independence, literature need not bear the weight of having to be "Christian" or "religious" in order to be of interest and value to the believer. Clearly, literature is not cut off from what believers hold to be important, since after all it does fall under God's broad, preserving care of the earth and its people. Thinking of its independence, we can approach literature with some objectivity, noting what literary people expect of good literature, observing the standards that have seemed to work over the ages, reading the text carefully, paying attention to the context, using our minds and imaginations. For all that objectivity, however, our own experiences and opinions are not put aside while we read: that could only be the case if we separated God's two ways of guiding and pretended we could be Christians one minute and rational critics the next without any connection between the two. We are both at once: believers in the sufficiency of God's boundless love, and limited creatures looking anywhere we can for a little wisdom to get through the next day. We are both people of faith and objective, serious readers and critics. If we take seriously our dual role as believer and citizen, we will study national political issues and try to make those complicated decisions with good reason and as much clarity about the task as we can muster. If we take seriously our role as believer and reader-critic, we might well try to understand how to make literary judgments—also how to read, how to imagine.

2

IMAGINING

Once upon a time there was a small white rabbit. She was furry [as rabbits are wont to be] and very inquisitive. She liked to hop around and explore her woods and visit other animals and fancy herself sometimes a matchgirl, sometimes a queen, sometimes a corporate executive. She really hadn't settled on what she wanted to be: the possibilities seemed endless.

One winter day, as she was sitting in her favorite place wedged between a large, snow-covered rock and a giant tree, she heard a dreadful racket behind her. Peeping between the rock and the tree, careful to keep her camouflage, she saw a fierce bobcat [they are always "fierce"] chasing a chipmunk. Rabbit didn't know whether to run for her own safety or to watch from her hiding place what she knew would be an awful slaughter. Or she could just close her eyes very tightly and clap her paws over her ears.

Before she could even decide what to do, and just as the bobcat caught up with the chipmunk, a great bird flew down at the bobcat, startling him and making him let the chipmunk go in order to fight the flurry of feathers and wings and talons that was attacking him. The bird looked beautiful to Rabbit, full of color and strength and energy. But then, with a mighty swoop of a paw, the bobcat knocked the great bird into the snow and pounced on it.

Rabbit could not watch. She saw only the scattering of purple feathers on the white snow, and she darted for home hoping the bobcat would be too busy with his prey to bother with a little rabbit. When she reached the warren, she began to blurt out what she had seen.

"What an imagination you do have!" said her mother.

"You've been daydreaming again," said her grandmother.

"I've been telling you, you watch too much television," her father growled—as close as he could come to a growl.

Rabbit went to her room and cried.

One of the problems we must face is that words like "imagination" and "metaphor" and "story" seem somehow to belong to the world of the untrue. In our culture we have been told that daydreaming is a waste of time; children have been warned against having too much imagination; some of us were even taught to read in the dull world of Dick and Jane and Spot. In the church we have sometimes been satisfied only when the liturgy has been followed to the letter, and we have considered Bible stories proper learning materials for children only. "Story" somehow for us has come to suggest falsehood, as in "telling a story," "telling a fib"; "story" suggests something made up by someone, a product of a person's fancy and, therefore, not sufficiently grounded in reality to be true. Such attitudes may spring from our Puritan heritage, where imaginative literature was often regarded as both a waste and danger, or from our technological society, where facts are basic and scientific method rules. Despite the prevailing inclinations, I will argue that imagination and story are the very stuff of truth.

In the first chapter, I talked about God's care of everything that is, everything we know and experience on this earth. Literature appropriately belongs under the way God cares as creator and preserver: it exists as an independent field with its own laws and principles. We do not expect it to save us, though it can help us to get along in the world; it can, we might say, prime us for wholeness. In this chapter, I look at the role of the reader, specifically at the reader's imagination and beliefs. Since literature is an independent field under God's plan for preserving the earth, believers and nonbelievers alike will approach it with the same basic set of tools—and we will talk about those tools in the next chapter. We must now ask what difference, if any, it makes that the reader is also a Christian; and we must ask how an understanding of the role of the imagination can help us clarify a relationship between literature and theology.

A DEFINITION OF IMAGINATION

Entire books have been written about the imagination.[1] For our purposes here, however, I propose that we regard the imagination as the mind's capacity for transferring our attention from one set of realities to another. This is to say that imagination, far from being a flight from the things of this earth, is indeed grounded in reality and actual concrete experience; it has to do with a process that our minds perform and so is a kind of thinking. It is necessarily related to the work of our senses and so is a kind of feeling. When the imagination is active, we move mentally from one reality to another, sometimes from the concrete and specific toward memories or pictures in our minds, sometimes from a word on a page or a picture in our minds toward the concrete and specific.

The imagination can carry us into the past. For example, I walk near a beach and I see a palmetto leaf that is quite real. If I jabbed the end of a leaf into my finger, the leaf would draw red blood; if I ran my hand along its flat surface, I would feel the ridges of the leaf; if I pulled it from its tree and waved it in front of my face, I would feel its breeze. I might think, then, of what a good fan such a leaf would be and of taking a pair of scissors and cutting off outer reaches of the section so that I would be left with the central, close-knit semicircle and so with one firm object for fanning. I might also recall fans I remember from my grandmother's house and her little country church, fans that were cardboard and had on one side the design of a palmetto leaf and on the other the name of a funeral home and, for a handle, a flat wooden stick like a giant's tongue depressor. This fan I see only in my imagination, we might say, but it is not less real for all that. My mind has carried me from a present and specific observation to a cherished memory—all in a matter of a few seconds—and, without being terribly conscious of it, I have been exercising my imagination.

The process can also lead us into closer touch with daily realities. I read a book about a woman and her two daughters: one of the daughters has the same name as my own daughter, and she reflects on the memory of her now-deceased father.[2] I cannot help but think, as I read, of my own daughter, who is now downstairs playing the piano, and of my relationship with her. The story in the book and the characteristics of that daughter and father are quite different from our story and characteristics, but the words on the page have carried me, in my mind, out of the book and back to my daily routine, to the concrete reality of my experience.

The imagination can move us, furthermore, from ordinary perceptions to new awareness and understanding. Perhaps as I read Gail Godwin's description of a father and his daughter, I not only reflect on my relationship with my own daughter; I may also begin to see new ways our lives could be strengthened and nourished. Perhaps, as I think about fans and palmetto leaves, my mind leaps to some new way of enduring hot weather, some new cooling device. The imagination prompts inventions and discoveries, as the mind jumps from what is to what might be, from a present difficult problem to a possible solution. What if we could talk to one another across hundreds of miles? What if we could fly? What if we could store information in a technological brain and recall it by pressing a button? The mind's movement from one set of realities to another makes for human creativity and caregiving.

We do not have to make our minds perform in these ways. The imagination in this busy, continuous process, is always at work to bring together present, past, and future, the immediate and the distant. That is the way our systems, our brains, seem to function; and it is an amazing pattern, at the very heart of our existence as creatures on this earth. Sometimes we have absolutely no control over the process, and the memories and pictures pop into our minds one after the other, like a fast-paced slide show, and we can barely guess what will come next: that is part of our limitation as creatures. Sometimes we do control the process by concentrating on a particular set of images or a specific problem and making our minds bring up pictures from their store-houses and order them for some purpose, such as telling a story: that is part of our potential as creatures.

Imagination, then, is grounded in reality, rooted in the very stuff of life. It makes no difference whether the picture is immediately or substantially before us—as is the candle on my table—or existing in our minds, the thousand candles of birthday cakes and church altars and electrical power failures. The imagination works on the basis of reality; it has nothing else. To be sure, the imagination might also lose touch with reality: a person might imagine being a Ty Cobb or a Hank Aaron, might abandon everyday responsibilities and live in another world, a world perhaps false and destructive to the people around that person. Such a possibility too is a consequence of our existence as limited creatures, a combination of creative gift with damaging experience, like high- and low-pressure areas slamming into one another. That our imaginations can run out of control does not suggest that we should constantly struggle to keep them in check; the imagination is, after all, an essential part of our existence as creatures of this earth, and so one of God's major gifts to us. The genuine human functioning of the imagination involves its free movement from one reality to another; in some sense our own wholeness as human beings is defined by that free movement. That wholeness can be broken, is broken time and again, and the imagination is destroyed. The imagination can be destroyed when it becomes an end in itself and the mind no longer moves freely among the realities but moves steadily away from the present, earthbound, tough realities of our lives. That is escape. The imagination can also be destroyed when it is abandoned, when we try to concentrate entirely on the concrete things of this earth and resist the free play of the mind, when we try to live only by the facts. That is a kind of death. The imagination can be destroyed when it is submitted to the control of some power outside our own wills—when, for example, we allow a television set to provide all our pictures for us, and we focus so entirely on this succession of images that our mind has no space for its own free play, and we risk losing the gift. That is atrophy.

When the imagination is destroyed, we are ourselves broken creatures, but the destruction does not just happen to us as though we were the victims of some fate. Rather, we deny the free movement of our minds, prefer some pattern other than that recommended by the creator; we no longer trust the creator's gift. That is sin.

GOD'S GIFT OF IMAGINATION

As a gift of God, imagination is one of the basic characteristics of the human being and is available to all God's human creatures whether or not they trust or acknowledge the giver. It is one of the things which distinguishes us from other animals on this earth. It is part of what we mean when we talk in the church about the "image of God": we can imagine just as God can imagine; we too can make images, have pictures in our minds, and cause these pictures to come alive and make a difference in the world. When I talked above about God's two ways of caring and about our own lives under both those patterns, I pointed to the danger of dividing ourselves into two parts that were inconsistently and falsely separated, and I argued for the unity we usually experience. Perhaps the imagination will give us a clearer means of expressing that essential unity.

We are creatures of imagination. Our minds work, in part, by enabling us to move freely from one set of realities to another across the broadest possible range of our experiences. God the creator made us that way; God the preserver sustains our lives that way, giving us pleasure and nourishment and balance. In no way can we conclude, however, that the imagination is a gift belonging only to God's creator/preserver way of giving care; just as surely, God the divine lover/present forgiver guides through the imagination as well. There is no wall within our minds separating our imagination into two different parts, and no sieve through which pictures must be squeezed for some determination of their relative "holiness" or "worldliness." We are single beings, creatures of imagination, using our imaginations both as we live in this world and as we live in the church. We do not have two imaginations, one for the world, another for the church;

rather, we have one imagination constantly transferring pictures, experiences, memories, and hopes in the context of all our activities.

I have already spoken of how the imagination functions in the area of the creation; we are accustomed to letting it have its way there. But think now about how the imagination works in the area of wholeness or redemption, of God's way of giving care through love and acceptance. In this area, we are perhaps less familiar with thinking about the work of the imagination, since, at least at some points in our history, "imagination" has suggested something less than real. We have seen, though, that imagination is based solidly on reality in the created order, and so it rests there as well in God's guidance of our lives as believers.

As one of God's gifts, to help us accept God's love and trust God's caregiving, the imagination helps us move from events of history to confidence in God's direction of history and from present daily experience to the experience of God's daily presence. Just as much as in the created order, the imagination here too is grounded in reality. The great story of God's activity in the drama of the people of Israel provides one concrete acting out of reality—an acting out that the imagination helps us put together and interpret. Our imaginations work on biblical stories in much the same way we might work on any other stories; the difference is that in the biblical accounts we uncover a consistent theme—so consistent that it appears to be the intention of the writers to make it stand out among all the diversity of the material.

This biblical theme can be stated best in story form: the very God who made all that is loves the people of this earth so much as to rescue them over and over again, to declare them a special and holy nation, and finally to take on human form, experience the agonies of the created order, and bring to all the creatures the invitation and the gift of wholeness and new life. Such a theme is acted out in the story of the people of Israel coming from slavery in Egypt—a story that is constantly repeated in the various biblical narratives. It is acted out in the stories of the prophets who sensed, on the basis of the history of God's relationship with Israel, that God is a god of inclusive love who will rule all of history and one day turn the world around toward wholeness and peace. It is acted out in the life story of Jesus of Nazareth, whose own imagination played so freely with both the things of creation and the promise of love that his own identity with God was clear to those who followed him. The great divine imagination is rolled together in one free and loving outburst on a weekend in Palestine, transferring death to life both in the divine mind's eye and on a real-life, stormy hillside, with a real wooden cross of execution and a really empty tomb; transferring death to life as well in the vivid experience and memory of a group of real-life people who knew they had seen the ancient promise finally enacted in the history of this God-human person. The theme is further worked out in the continuing narrative of those very people whose imaginations were fired by a confidence that God's rule on earth had indeed begun and that God had demonstrated a new way of guiding and caring, a way of love and wholeness. They imagined that they were the instruments of such guidance. They were not drunk, nor were they carried away from reality into illusion. God also imagined them that way, and God's good news was carried from person to person, from town to town, and the church was launched into the world.

In order to hear that story or to tell it, we depend on our imaginations, a gift of God. We might say that God reveals the story using human imaginations, or that the imagination is a vehicle for revelation. In his *St. Joan*, George Bernard Shaw (certainly no orthodox theologian of the church) presents this exchange between Joan of Arc and one of her inquisitors:

> Joan: I hear voices telling me what to do. They come from God.
> Robert: They came from your imagination.
> Joan: Of course! That is how the message of God comes to us.[3]

Now, we may feel uneasy with Joan's response because we prefer our revelations to be objective and external to us and unambiguous. And yet is revelation ever so objective and unambiguous in our experience? Faith hears and trusts God's Word; doubt worries and questions. We live with that faith-doubt tension. If the understanding of the imagination presented here has any merit, furthermore, it reminds us that the imagination is grounded in the concrete, and it helps us to see how God reveals, unveils, unfolds the divine strategies by using concrete realities and also by using our minds' capacity for transferring from one reality to another.

So this God-gift of imagination enables us to move from the earthy narratives of the Bible to assurance of the deeper reality that those narratives convey, and it enables us to move from this deeper reality back into our daily lives for the decisions and pleasures and actions that are ours there. No difference appears in the way our imaginations work under this pattern of God's guidance: the difference lies in the promise that is clearly tied to the experiences of this pattern. The promise guides the movement of those realities being shifted around in our minds. God is speaking to us in that promise of love, and God uses the most ordinary means to get the message across: a splash of water, a taste of bread and wine, the human voices of friends and pastors in the church, the ink and paper of a Bible, even the tainted record of the church's history. In that splash of water, God imagines us whole and pure, and we imagine ourselves God's own children, awake again to that healing love. To say "we imagine ourselves" is not to say that we "pretend" it is true, or that we "think" it so even though we know it really isn't. Imagination is grounded in reality. With this promise from God, the water is one way for us to grab hold of that reality, and God's Word of love is another.

Our imaginations may not always make the connections God would like them to make. Certainly, those who do not trust God as divine lover and present forgiver will see only a splash of water during a ritual which they will consider primarily one of society's methods of welcoming a child to earth and giving a name. Yet as we place ourselves where we can hear the promise—as we return Sunday after Sunday to that community wherein the stories are told, the water splashed, the bread and wine taken in as nourishment—just there are our imaginations quickened, our trust restored, our lives made whole again and again. Our problems and decisions are still working in our minds; yet we hear again, through all that, God's promise of love. For us to hear the promise, under real conditions, our imaginations have to be working overtime; God must be working too.

Thus, the imagination works both under God's care of the whole society through those divine creative powers and under God's care of believers through the expressions of accepting love. Within the creation, the imagination helps us see the world with eyes other than our own; it involves us closely with the things of the earth; it reminds us of our limitations and gives us confidence in our abilities. Within the creation, the imagination is built upon the world.[4] Within the way of healing love, the imagination is also dependent on the things of the earth, but it is built now on both God's world and God's Word. It leads to the deeper reality of God's loving promises; it leads to confidence in God's Word. In the way of creation, the imagination leads to creative action; in the way of love, it leads to faith. If it is distorted and becomes an end in itself, it works against God in both areas: in creation, it can become utopian and idealistic; in the way of love, it can become ecstasy, spiritualism, otherworldliness.[5] Without the imagination, writings in the area of creation become dull treatises, mechanical prescriptions; with it, they become poetry; without it, writings in the area of restoring love become dead dogma, lifeless sermonic performances; with it, they become gracious good news. The imagination is a human capability, but it is also consistently God's gift. We do not summon our imaginative powers and so invent God's love; rather, God loves and cares and gives us the capacity to imagine that the divine love and care is present and active for us. The Word bears that promise to us.

Again, lest we forget: we live under both patterns of caregiving at once, so our imaginations are constantly at work in both areas. This means again that we live in tension and ambiguity; life is never quite as clear or as easy as we might wish. Tension, however, is not always the destructive force we think of when, for example, we talk about "tension headaches." Tension is also the tightness of a tennis racket's strings, a tightness that enables the player to place a ball across the net; it is the pull of a bowstring that will send an arrow toward its target; it is even the tautness of a clothesline that keeps the sheets from dragging in the dirt; it is the excitement of a good film or novel. Tension spells trouble at times, but it also signals pleasure and adventure. Strange as it may seem, God's tension is good news, an invitation to life.

We have perhaps been speaking so far as though either the imagination were the final object on our horizons or, more likely, as though we ourselves were that final object: the imagination, under both God's plans, comes to us. We find ourselves loaded up with it. How then are we to use imagination? One thing we will talk about is using imagination as we read literature. But another point, broader in scope than the reading of literature, needs mention here and will be developed later on: imagination doesn't come pouring out on us so that we can soak it up and revel in it; God's gift of imagination has more purpose than that. We have seen that the imagination enables us to hear and trust God's Word and to understand and shape God's world; in a way, that is God's gift aimed toward each of us individually. As we receive that gift, we also get a commission. Again, we can think of the commission operating under each plan of caregiving, as well as in some unified way. Under the plan of guidance for accepting love, we use the imagination to proclaim the gospel, to be priests and servants, taking what we know of the Word and making such vivid pictures that others can see it as well. Under the plan of guidance for preservation, we use the imagination to be citizens and poets, taking what we see of the world and making such vivid pictures that others also can both understand and shape the world—as we are all asked to do—and begin to plan and enact ways to change it. This is really part of the shaping, for by imaginative shaping I mean not merely molding clay into pottery or words into poetry but also facing up to the weak and corrupt institutions of our society and shaping them for justice and peace.

The point is that imagination does not work simply for our own pleasure or for such distinct activities as writing sermons and composing short stories; rather, the imagination works too to address real human needs as part of God's preserving and loving plans. We are then caught in the middle again: prophets, in a way, announcing that God is both lover and preserver, building strategies that will make us also agents of both love and preservation. Believers find themselves on just such a field, a field that becomes at once battleground and parade ground.

IMAGINATION IN THE RELATIONSHIP
BETWEEN LITERATURE
AND THEOLOGY

If the imagination provides a means for us to understand the unity of our lives under both God's caretaking plans, perhaps it will also help us carry further an analysis of the relationship between literature and theology. I have said that literature is an independent field under the area of God's care for all things as creator and preserver; that the reader who is a Christian uses the same critical tools as does anyone else in evaluating a piece of literature; and that the imagination works in the same fashion for both believer and nonbeliever. If all that is true, what does the Christian do when he or she reads a modern short story? What happens when one encounters allusions that are specifically religious? What happens when one reads a story written by someone who claims to be a Christian? Aren't there some special rules, after all? If we live in both God's territories at once, and if our imaginations are constantly moving between the two, don't we need some special rules for a Christian interpretation of literature?

So far, I have resisted terms like "Christian interpretation," "Christian reader," "Christian critic," and even "religious literature" or "Christian literature." I shall continue to resist. Such terms only muddy already troubled waters and are extremely difficult to use with any precision because so few people will agree about what they mean. "Religion" can mean anything from a warm feeling about life to belief in some kind of god to an institution dedicated to one of those two. It can mean at least something like that, and it can mean, more broadly perhaps, the aspiration of the human for the divine. "Christian" has some of the same problems for many people in our culture, since it often seems to be completely synonymous with "religion" or to be a subdivision of religion. Under such definitions, it is meaningless to talk about "religious literature" or even "Christian literature." Almost any piece of writing could be placed under the first term, under the second any piece of writing that includes some specific reference to a theme or symbol familiar within Christianity. So what is wrong with that? Not an enormous amount, I suppose, but it is certainly not precise use of language, and it does not help us move toward clarity.

It might be much more helpful if we use the term "religious literature" to refer only to writings that are specifically related to some religious movement; so sacred texts, scriptures, hymns, prayers, tracts, sermons might be labeled religious literature. Thus, the Koran is religious literature, the Gospel of Mark is Christian literature; guidelines for transcendental meditation would be religious literature, as would Kahlil Gibran's *The Prophet* and a mosque prayer; a hymn by Charles Wesley or a sermon by Jonathan Edwards would be Christian literature. Within each category one might argue about the relative orthodoxy of the work according to standards appropriate to that category. Other literature—a novel from India, or a short story from Great Britain, for example—might have within it religious allusions or themes, Hindu or Christian symbols; but we would not have to decide on some totally unmanageable basis whether or not the novel or short story were itself somehow religious or Christian or Hindu. Such an arrangement would be neater than the confusion of terms we must now face.

The world, however, is not so neat. What are we to do, for instance, when a believer writes a short story and markets it not in the church, as perhaps an illustration for a church school lesson, but in the world's marketplace alongside other stories by nonbelievers? Someone like Flannery O'Connor would be a good example of such a situation, as would T. S. Eliot in his later works or C. S. Lewis. From the other side of the page, what are we to do when as believers we find what seems to us unmistakable echoes of our faith in the writings of a nonbeliever? Do we then claim that writer for our side, perform a baptism of sorts? Wouldn't that, then, be Christian literature? The world is not very neat.

All along we have said that we live our lives not either in the church or in the world but in both church and world. There can be no neat compartmentalizing of faith and work. In some instances, it may even be difficult to tell believer from nonbeliever. Mere churchgoing or public confessions would not be enough, hypocrisy being what it is; perhaps not even absence from church or public dismissal of faith would be a guarantee, since only God knows the human heart. Can we tell the Bible from other works of literature? Is the canon closed: could some modern short story which accurately proclaims God's love someday be included in another collection following the Revelation to John? If so, wouldn't it be Christian literature, and why isn't it now?

Nothing is to be gained by rigidity and legalism on this issue. If it pleases someone to call a work by T. S. Eliot or Flannery O'Connor "Christian literature," then nothing is likely to stop them from using the term, and perhaps not much harm is done. The point is that the terminology ultimately is not helpful. Once you set up a category, then you might look around for things to put in it. Maybe we would agree about Eliot and O'Connor, but what about John Updike or William Faulkner or James Joyce (all writers whose stories have allusions to Christian or biblical themes and images)? Would we include all of Eliot or just certain pieces? How exactly would we decide what goes in and what stays out? If I may have my tension again, I will not draw rigid lines separating some literature from other on the basis of the degree of faith it shows or the number of allusions with Christian content; nor will I want all the the lines to be wiped away. I prefer to live with the tension, reading the Bible with one hand and Faulkner— or O'Connor—with the other. Sometimes the Bible and literature may be close together in what they are saying, but I will be confident that the Word, with the promise attached, is dependably from God and expresses God's amazing love; and I will rest easy with the ambiguity of the word from the writer who may well prepare me to hear God's Word anew.

When the reader who is a Christian comes across a piece of literature, what specific tasks of interpretation will he or she perform? That reader will be doing what any other reader would be doing, examining the text closely, studying its background and its author, tracking down allusions and archetypes, noting dominant images and all the rest (we will review these tasks in the next chapter). In other words, this reader too will attempt to be a responsible literary critic using the best skills of that field of study. There is no such thing as "Christian literary criticism."[6] The differences between readers who are Christians and those who are not will lie only in the readers themselves, as individuals with their own distinct education and up-bringing and experience. The reader who is Christian, for example, may have a good knowledge of the Bible and so may be quick to catch biblical allusions. Or familiarity with points of Christian doctrine may enable this reader to detect when a character in a story is supporting or denying some doctrinal emphasis. Or membership in a certain denomination may mean that this reader will feel some identity if one of the characters also is associated with that denomination—or be able to offer some correction if the writer (or the character) seems to have misunderstood that particular group of Christians. None of this makes this reader a better critic than another person who might not acknowledge God as creator and preserver but who has other personal resources to aid in the business of interpretation. The other reader, the nonbeliever, may more easily identify with nonbelievers in the fiction, may know Greek mythology better, may be more widely read in other fields, and so forth.

The reader is one of the imaginative pieces of this puzzle, and each reader will bring to the task of solving the puzzle a personal set of memories, experiences, beliefs, and a certain body of learned material. This is the subjective element in criticism. The reader who is a Christian simply brings a different set of experiences: in some cases, those experiences will mean some advantage for the interpreter; in other cases, they may even prove to be a hindrance. If this reader who is a Christian has any advantage, it may be a slight guard against self-righteousness in interpretation, since he or she will have recognized the ambiguity of human experience and the limitations of personal authority. The record shows, however, that even in matters of literary criticism the Christian can be just as arrogant and self-assured as anyone else and sometimes claims divine approval to boot.

A reader who is a Christian may sometimes want so badly to find in contemporary fiction some kindred spirit or some sign of the world's approval of the faith that he or she might be much too quick to interpret references positively, that is, to interpret them as affirming his or her personal belief. As long as you keep your judgments to yourself or to your circle of friends, probably little harm is done by this possessiveness of a work of literature for the faith. If you mean to publish your judgment, though, you may well damage your credibility, along with that of other Christians, unless you have done your homework solidly and can support your conclusions from the text itself. This caution applies to the use of literature in the sermon as well as to other critical discussions such as book reviews or essays. The preacher abuses literature and does a disservice to members of the congregation when he or she simply snatches a reference from a literary work with no attention to the context of the reference or the overall meaning of the narrative. By the same token, the preacher who reads contemporary fiction carefully and lets it prompt his or her imagination may not only sharpen the proclamation of the Word but may also awaken the imagination of the hearers of the sermon both to the Word and to the possible benefits of contemporary literature. That preacher may have a clearer impression as well of the thoughts and feelings of the people who listen to the sermon. Let the literature do its proper work of entertaining and informing, and build conclusions on the evidence of the text.

How will you know if your interpretation is correct? You may feel that you have read carefully and studied the necessary background materials, but you will remain aware of the subjective nature of your conclusions. I'm telling you to trust yourself and not to trust yourself—more contradictions! First, there is no guaranteed, absolutely correct, infallible meaning to a story or its parts. Second, if you've treated the text faithfully, you have a good chance of being on the right track. Third, try your opinions out on someone else. Reading alone may not be as dangerous as swimming alone, but it will have its hazards. Find another group of people who like to read, and dig in together. You will get benefits other than just second opinions on your interpretation; you will also have the advantage of the subjective reaction and experience and memory of other readers, and the literature may yield even more, under those conditions, than you first expected. I will say more about such a community of readers in chapter 5, but first I must examine those tasks by which a reader analyzes a text. What sort of objective steps might we take to offer some control on our subjective imaginations? How do you allow the imagination its freedom and playfulness and still be faithful to the printed text before you? What is an appropriate balance between that text and your own imagination?

3

INTERPRETING

When we consider how we are to read and understand a literary text, given our assumption that literature is an independent field not dominated by theology, we realize that we are to use the same principles and methods that literary critics use. One's trust in God has nothing to do with how he or she reads a work of literature. The reader who is a Christian will analyze a text with exactly the same tools used by the reader who is not a Christian, and the success of the analysis will depend not upon the faith of the reader but the skill with which those tools are used. Having said that, we must also acknowledge that we still face enormous difficulties, since literary critics are by no means in any agreement about how one should analyze a text or what one can or should say about a text or what one might expect from a text. Such confusion among the scholars leaves in even more of a muddle those readers who have limited literary or critical training. Toward which critics should one turn for guidance?

In view of this confusion, we might be tempted to ignore the critics altogether. After all, we know what we like: why shouldn't we read what we enjoy and say what we want about it? An independent spirit clearly fits our pragmatic culture and may even draw some support from a Protestant insistence on the authority of the individual conscience. In one way, no one can argue against it: who is to stop any reader from reading and judging as he or she wills? Taste is not easily influenced. We change reading habits and critical opinions very slowly, if at all, and we are quick to defend our own preferences. But the problem with this individualistic approach is that we may well miss out on some of what literature has to offer. We can only see from one angle, from the limits of our own experience; and if our experience is limited—and it always is to some degree—then we will miss some of the possibilities. Readers who read only for the story—that is, to follow the development of the plot—may not stop to think about allusions and symbols; and those who read searching for allusions may never really have a sense of what the whole work is about. To know some literary principles of criticism and to hear what others— either scholars or ordinary readers—have thought about a text can only enrich our own reading.

The path through the maze of modern literary criticism is too circuitous for detailed exploration here.[1] What we need at this point is not a survey of critical theories but guidance in the reading and criticism of literature. Much is to be learned from a number of critics, and we need not limit ourselves to one approach. In this chapter I will discuss a number of fundamental issues that any interpreter might consider, and I will suggest some guidelines with which any reader might experiment. I operate on the assumption that we do not need to follow one particular critical position but may learn that we can from several different approaches. These suggestions cannot be followed mechanically, without careful thought and imagination. They are only recommendations for your own reading.

In trying to understand any poem or story, we come close to our goal as we learn something about the text itself, the author, the background of the text—that is, the time it was written, other ex- pressions in a similar form, the history of its criticism—and, not least, about ourselves. At different periods of time, critical theory has em- phasized one of these areas, sometimes to the exclusion of the others. Three-quarters of a century ago, literature was taught through its background, and one tried to learn something about the historical situation that might have prompted the piece, something of the so- ciological context, something of the author's biography and other writings. Along the way it was not surprising that the work itself almost got lost. Then some critics, reacting against such an approach, argued that the text itself was most important, after all, and all the reader needed to do was read carefully, paying attention to each word, every sentence, nuances of punctuation, and shades of meaning. It mattered not what was happening in history or what the author had been experiencing; all that mattered were the words and form of the text itself. Although this was a valuable corrective to what had been the earlier pattern, it was soon found to be quite limiting. Sometimes, for example, a particular poem might not seem to mean anything unless the reader had some knowledge of its background and context. That would be all right, argued some critics, since it is enough that a work of art exists: we need not worry about what it might mean, and if it should mean nothing that would be all right too. Lately, still other critics have reminded us that the reader is surely not to be overlooked. Each reader brings personal experiences to any work of literature; private connotations for a particular word, personal memories that may parallel or stand in sharp contrast with the events or characters of the work. Each reader has a set of personal opinions, beliefs, and values that will necessarily influence how the work is interpreted. The critics who insisted on the background or the text as primary were inclined to forget the role of the reader, as though the reader were somehow a neutral element within the process. A number of contemporary interpreters are pointing out that the interpretive task cannot be complete, cannot be performed, without the reader and whatever experiences the reader brings to the reading. As we work toward some guidelines for interpretation, therefore, we will want to consider each of these four areas: text, background, author, and reader.

Before I take up these areas and work toward a method of interpretation, I should clarify once more my basic intentions. I can do that best by saying what I am *not* doing here. For one thing, I am not trying to outline the proper method for scholarly interpretation of a work of literature. Literary scholars will have time for more exhaustive study and research, and though they may consider the same items listed below, they will no doubt undertake their analysis at more depth and will perhaps have more steps in the process. My concern centers on how people who are not professional students of literature may read and understand and feel some confidence about what they are doing. Any professional woodworker can, it should be obvious, do a more exact, smoother job of building a cabinet than an amateur, and in less time. Still, if the amateur observes the woodworker in action and reads some things about techniques and practices enough on her own, she may be able to turn out a fairly respectable job, that is, one that is satisfying to her and useful in her home. It may be tempting to assume that since most readers have been through some years of formal education they need not have additional training in such an elementary experience of life as reading fiction. My suspicion, however, is that many people have had little practice interpreting a piece of literature since school days, that whatever basic critical tools they once knew and used have been forgotten, and that people tend to let others interpret for them. (For example, we may depend on pastors and church school teachers to interpret the Bible for us, considering them the professional critics and assuming that they alone have the needed skills for the task.) I suspect that some readers may even prefer not bothering with interpretation: "Don't ask me what something means; just tell me, or let me enjoy it without thinking too hard about it." Not all of my suspicions will apply to each reader, of course, but they may apply to some. My conviction is that most of us can not only benefit from reading and understanding literature but can develop, without too much difficulty, the competence to make satisfying and responsible interpretations.

What follows will not be a series of steps that can be followed one by one to arrive automatically at a correct interpretation of any piece of literature. Maybe that is too evident to need stating, but since we seem to have a passion for how-to guides in our country, I want to be sure we understand that these guidelines cannot fall into such a category. I am offering here no magic formula. Literature is much too intricate for that; meaning is too rich and subtle; the tasks of interpretation are too varied and interpenetrating. The difficulties should be even plainer as we move along, for we will see that one element of a work of literature (a symbol, for example) can never really be separated from another (development of a character, for example). Arriving at some sense of the meaning of the symbol has so much to do with the way the symbol is worked out at other places in the literature, how it might be used in other literature of our heritage, what shades of meaning that word may have for each of us individually, and so on. At every step of the way, we are looking ahead to what more is to come, backward at what we have already understood, and to the right and left to see what else around us might affect the current judgments. I acknowledge that this sounds complicated; but we can read and come to conclusions, though they may at times be tentative or ambiguous ones. Through the process of analysis and dialogue and inquiry, the benefits of the literature become clearer—and that, after all, was the goal at the beginning.

THE TEXT

To begin the discussion by talking about what we do to and with the text itself is to start with the centerpiece of the interpretive task.[2] Those critics who called us back to the text were right in reminding us of the text's central place, even if they were wrong in excluding other matters from the reader's attention. The particular story (or poem or drama—but for simplicity we will talk only of story) that we read has its own existence: its words are arranged on the pages in a certain order and with certain implications. In some sense, that particular story is independent. It stands there asking for our examination, our interest, our questions, our responses, our amusement, and our enjoy-ment. The author—we will get to the author in a later section—has just these characters with just these traits, has used these particular words and images, has developed the action in just this way. Readers, of course, may disagree about the character traits, the meaning of the words and images, the consequences of the action; but in order to discuss any of those elements or come to any meaningful dialogue about them, the readers must examine the text, the words on the page. Unless the characters are all stereotypes, the images and symbols all highlighted, the ideas all propaganda, the action all straightforward—and some fiction has those features—unless all that is true, a work will have ambiguity and plenty of room for mixed judgment by its readers. If a story is totally unmistakable in all of its dimensions, we are left with very little to talk about—if we are still awake enough to talk.

If we set out to interpret a particular story, we can begin at any number of entry points. To some degree, it will not matter where we begin, since we will eventually get around to the other steps, and each will build upon another. In fact, as we approach a story, we may not even know which would be the most incisive entry point; so we dig in somewhere, follow the leads as best we can, and then move on to another element. When we have covered all the elements that seem applicable, then we step back and try to put things together, try to see the story as a whole, and come to some conclusions.

Character

Sometimes it is the characters of the story who most engage our imaginations. We come to meet them as we would new friends: we get to know them—in limited ways to be sure—and we grow to like them or despise them. We may begin to see life, for a time, through the eyes of this other new person, and we have to decide if we can trust the character's judgment and if we respect or agree with his or her way of looking at things. If we are to interpret a story, therefore, we will make some decisions about the characters in the story. We will iden-tify which are the main characters and which appear in supporting roles. If two or more characters seem to dominate the action, we can ask which seems most central to the action and ideas, and we can identify ways in which they may be set over against one another. We can also ask if any of the characters are stereotypes: that is, we can attempt to determine if a character comes across as a real and believ-able person, with the agonizing changes of opinion and the unex-pected patterns of behavior we see in ourselves and in our neighbors, or if the character is entirely predictable. Literary critics call stereo-typed characters "flat" because they don't have much depth of development, and when you first meet them you know exactly how they will conduct themselves throughout the story. A writer can portray with very few strokes, for instance, the figure of what we have come to think of as the typical Southern sheriff: someone who is overweight, gruff, and highly prejudiced, and who speaks substandard English in a slow drawl. Most of us know that not many Southern sheriffs are actually like that, but we will recognize the type as soon as the writer gives us just a few of the features; we can fill in the blanks from our own imaginations and experiences. A writer will often use a "flat" character in a minor role and count on the reader to accept that character as a stereotype: the character is not important enough for more complete development but can still serve a function in the story. If all the characters in a story are altogether predictable, our imaginations have little to do, we are not much stimulated, and the writer has probably produced a weak and uninteresting narrative.

We learn about the characters in a variety of ways. We can study the character herself: for example, watch her mannerisms, listen to what she says and thinks about herself. We may be able to learn about her by what other characters in the novel say or by how the narrator describes her. In this sort of character analysis, of course, we must decide whom we can believe. Is the character reliable? We will wonder if we can trust her judgment about herself (she may be deceiving herself) or her judgment about other characters (she may have reason to deceive us about them). We can also look for words associated with the character: perhaps some color is mentioned whenever the character appears, or some striking image—a bird or flower or machine—or some distinct emotion.

In John Gardner's novel *The Resurrection*, for example, one character is named Viola, and the word "violence" appears repeatedly in proximity to her name.[3] The use of such distinctive words around a character may be one of the ways the narrator or author has of giving us hints about the character, and they still will be among the building blocks we use to arrive at an analysis of who this person is and how she functions in the story.

As we examine a well-developed character, we are often taking deep steps into the human personality. We may find ourselves faced with questions we have not wanted to consider about ourselves. We may, depending on our own makeup, even be embarrassed at points: we may feel that we are facing dark secrets, too private to be spoken aloud. Sometimes this may be because the character is expressing or experiencing feelings we too have had and buried. Perhaps the character's story is our own story, and perhaps by seeing how her story works out, we may be getting some hints about our own future. This is one of the ways literature helps us comprehend more about ourselves, but such discovery may at times be painful. The distance we have from the character in the story, however, may help us face personal issues more honestly than we might with a counselor or friend; it may also enable us to ignore the issues and try to close the book and the memory at the same time. Literature is not a substitute psychologist, but it can, on occasion, set us on the road to discovery. This movement toward personal awareness is yet another part of understanding the characters in a story, and when we know the characters, we have one piece of information toward our interpretation of the story.

Plot

The plot of a story may seem at first glance to be the easiest element to follow. Most readers, we might assume, can tell what is happening in a narrative. Difficulties arise when the plot becomes extremely complicated, with so many twists and turns that even the most attentive reader may get lost along the way, or when the action of the story is so slight that the reader may have a feeling there is no plot. Some modern fiction seems much more interested in the development of ideas or characters than in the development of plot, in contrast to fiction of the nineteenth century with its intricate narrative sequences (for example, the novels of Scott or Dickens). A reader may feel that unless a story has a strong, action-filled plot it is not worth his or her time. Modern plotless stories may take some getting used to, but they will engage the mind on other levels if the reader will follow their approach to narrative.

No story is really plotless, of course; even a narrative made up entirely of a monologue by a single character, even the ramblings of a character's mind, will have some form to it. A character in a novel by Saul Bellow—*Herzog*, for example—may spend a lot of time thinking, dreaming, reminiscing, but those reflections will be related to what is still a strong story line.[4] Or there will seem to be not much action in a story like J. D. Salinger's *Franny and Zooey*, but the plot has to do with the interaction between the two main characters and what happens within each character.[5] Part of the process then is to identify the kind of fiction one is facing, to note how important the plot is to the overall story, and to decide what questions need to be asked about the sequence of events in the narrative.

Numerous questions will come to us. If a story mixes up time sequences with flashbacks or reports from the perspectives of separate characters, we may need to sort out the sequence of events. If a story takes place over an extended period of time, it may be helpful to work out a chronology of events. We might want to ask if the narrative's movement from one event to the other is clear and justified or if it should be; sometimes events in real life do not follow naturally and plainly from one another. If we are reading with a group of other persons, we may want to be sure we all have the same—or nearly the same—pictures of the basic plot structure. Is anyone puzzled about what happens at a given point in the story, and does that puzzle come from something within the narrative itself—some intricate sentences at key points of transition, or even some omission that the reader needed to fill in? Does the plot provide a base, a sense of balance for the whole narrative?[6] How does the plot relate to the development of the theme or characters or tone? With some stories we may not need to spend much time with analysis of plot, with others a great deal. In any case, this is one of the steps toward interpretation of a narrative.

Structure

By structure I mean something slightly different from plot. The plot has to do with the eventual forward movement of the story line from one point in time to another, from one experience of the characters to another. The structure has to do with the way the writer divides the material.

Almost any story will have some recognizable structure. A long and complicated novel may be divided into chapters and each chapter divided again into sections, sometimes marked clearly, sometimes only signaled by extra spaces between paragraphs. Even so short a narrative as Alice Walker's "The Welcome Table" has a well-defined structure, and attention to that structure helps with the interpretation, as will be seen in chapter 9 below. The reader can ask certain questions of a story in order to analyze its structure. Are there chapters within the story? Are there informal breaks in the narrative at which points the narrative's perspective changes or the normal time sequence is interrupted? Are we to understand that there is anything going on during those gaps—that is, does some time pass without our being told exactly what happens during that interval? Even if the writer does not identify these divisions in the text, it still might be possible for the reader to have some sense of the basic organization of a story. Trying to make an outline of that organization might be a useful way of fixing it in the mind.

Point of View

The reader is probably less conscious of the point of view of the story than of other elements such as plot and character. By point of view, we mean the perspective from which the story is told. Does the main character tell the story in the first person, so that you see the development in the narrative only through the eyes of that one character? Does the point of view change from one character to another, so that perhaps one chapter will be told through the mind of character A and the next through character B? Perhaps the story is told by the narrator, and all characters are spoken of in the third person. Even in the third person, though, the narrator may focus so closely on one character that you have a sense of seeing the story through that character's eyes—that is, the narrator will tell you what that character is thinking and feeling but will not let you in on the thoughts and feelings of any other characters. Or the story may be told by the narrator so that you know what each character is thinking and doing all along. This perspective is identified by the critics as the omniscient point of view, since the author, like God, knows everything in everyone's mind every step of the way. Some contemporary writers have abandoned this method of narration as unrealistic, since most human storytellers are able to see reality through only one pair of eyes (Henry James, writing at the turn of the twentieth century, was one of the first storytellers to urge this limited perspective). Another possibility, of course, is that the narrator will attempt to be perfectly neutral, to serve as a camera that records the actions without making any judgments; unless a character gives some verbal or visual display of emotion, we know no more about him than we would about another person we might see on the street, and we must observe all the more closely. Some of the Ernest Hemingway's stories illustrate this technique—as does Ernest Gaines's "A Long Day in November," which will be discussed in chapter 8.

Point of view is a versatile and fascinating tool for the writer and an important one for the reader to study. As we grasp the way perspective changes in a story or is used by the writer, we get additional information about the characters and the unfolding of events. In a story where multiple perspectives are presented, we are often able to compare one character's perception of events with another's and so find a more

secure basis for evaluating the credibility of each character. At times
we realize that we come close to the truth of a situation only as we
begin to gather all the various perspectives. William Faulkner's *Absalom, Absalom!* provides an exceptionally fine example of this, as we
read about incidents from the perspective of several different characters, no one of whom knows everything that happened, each searching
with us for clues to reality.[7]

Conflict

Most plots depend heavily on some kind of conflict. We might
almost say that without conflict there is no plot, nothing to keep the
action moving, nothing to engage a reader's interest about both the
characters and the situation. Conflict can appear in a story at a variety
of levels. We might witness a conflict between two characters, human
will set against human will, each vying with the other for dominance:
husband against wife, child against parent, neighbor against neighbor.
Sometimes this sort of conflict will be extended beyond the individual
to whole groups or clans. Such levels of conflict are fairly easy to
identify, and it is usually possible for us to tell who are the good
people and who are the bad. A little more subtle is the conflict that
goes on within the mind and experience of a single character: the
agonizing, the self-doubting, the battling of pride and guilt. Besides
these types of conflict, a story may develop conflict between ideas.
Such tension may be worked out by means of characters and situations
wherein a character, for example, comes to represent a set of ideas that
is opposed by the attitudes of other people in the story. As you read,
therefore, try to identify the types of conflict that seem to make the
narrative move forward; by stating those as precisely as possible, you
will apprehend the plot and characters and theme of the story more
clearly.

Allusions

An allusion is a reference by the writer to something—an idea,
image, symbol, place, or person—outside the story, or within the story
at some other point in the narrative. Often an allusion will lead the
reader to some other literature, perhaps to one of the classics of Greek
or Roman drama, or to Chaucer or Shakespeare, or to the Bible or
other sacred writings. The writer counts on the reader being able to
catch the allusion and know what was happening in the other literature and so let the earlier narrative add to the meaning in the story at
hand. If you find a reference with which you are not familiar, you will

have to do some investigation with a reference guide, encyclopedia, or dictionary if you are to make the most of the writer's hint. Allusions may cause us some discomfort by reminding us of our own limited background in other literature, but they most often enrich a story and enable the writer to establish a more universal thrust for the narrative. The allusion to some idea, symbol, image, place, or person within the story is an echo, a reminder to the reader of what has gone before, an author's way of pulling together narrative strands and providing threads of unity.

Images

Any story of almost any quality will be filled with images, with words and phrases that cause us to see pictures and hear sounds, to taste and touch and smell. Images are the writer's tools to bring reality to the printed page: they convince the reader that the story is grounded in the very stuff of this earth. Images add to the beauty of the language and help effect deeper levels of meaning and clarity. Consider this opening sentence from Alice Walker's story "The Welcome Table":

> The old woman stood with eyes uplifted in her Sunday-go-to-meeting clothes: high shoes polished about the tops and toes, a long rusty dress adorned with an old corsage, long withered, and the remnants of an elegant silk scarf as headrag stained with grease from the many oily pigtails underneath.[8]

The specific details of the sentence provide the pictures whereby we begin to envision the character; indeed, in that sentence almost every word is an image contributing to the larger description. The analysis of images may not seem to require much special attention, since images are fairly easy to identify. Nonetheless, the reader can learn a great deal from the way the author uses, builds, and controls the imagery of a story. The multiplication of images, like the accumulation of allusions, can work toward meaning or symbol or theme. Images also may push the reader deeply inward to what may appear to be hidden within the human experience but becomes more evident as we think and imagine the scene before us, as we let the imagery sink deeply into our own minds. What we look for is not necessarily every image that the writer uses but the way the images work together to establish the tone and make the characters believable and add to the levels of meaning within the story. The power of the imagery may also furnish means of evaluating a work of literature, inasmuch as we are likely to be more persuaded of the reality and depth of a work whose

images are more vivid and so carry us more effectively into the world
of the narrative.

Symbol

A symbol might work in somewhat the same way as an allusion
or an image: that is, it might supply pictures or broaden the dimensions of the story by reaching beyond the immediate events and
characters toward something more universal. A symbol points beyond
the present image and takes on a distinctive significance as a focus of
meaning for the narrative. It can tie a narrative together by appearing
at several key places in the story's development.[9] It gives us something
precise to think about;[10] it can open up to us, sometimes rather
suddenly, an awareness of how to understand the various episodes
unfolding before us.[11] We read in a story, for example, about a snake.
The first time the snake appears in the narrative, we may think very
little about it unless the writer has dramatized the appearance heavily
and makes it plain that the character is giving it a great deal of
attention. When the snake appears a second time, we will remember
the first and begin to get suspicious; if we have read very much at all
and know how frequently writers have made use of the snake as an
allusion to the Adam and Eve story, we will surely think of that
connection. As the snake slithers in again and again, we will realize
that the writer (or the characters) sees this as more than an ordinary
reptile and that kinship exists between this creature and the one in the
Garden of Eden. We may conclude that the snake before us is, indeed,
a symbol of evil. Not just any snake in any story can be taken so
seriously, of course. The possible symbolic value of the snake will
depend on how the writer develops it and whether it fits the rest of the
narrative for the snake to work as a symbol. Attention and engage-
ment, therefore, are required for analysis of symbols: they need to be
tested in context in the narrative. We must distinguish between symbol
and allusion. We can test for an ironic use of an image with symbolic
power. We need to be sure that the symbol actually functions within
the narrative we are reading and is not simply something that exists in
our minds, something we would like to find there. There is no automatic method of guaranteeing proper interpretation of symbols—
indeed, some of the pleasure in reading would evaporate if we had
such an automatic procedure. We can, however, expect that symbols
will appear in fiction, and we can attempt to get at their meaning
cautiously with scrutiny of the text itself.

Conventions

When we look for the conventions of a story, we are not trying to spot a gathering of characters at a grand hotel. "Convention" is one of those specialized literary terms; it refers to patterns that come to be repeated from one work of literature to another. Stereotypical characters—stock characters as they are sometimes called—would be one example of a convention: that is, such easily recognizable characters are a device used by many writers to draw a human portrait in a few strokes and so define for the reader a character whose role in the story needs to become immediately clear. The mere use of a convention is not a sign of inferior writing, of course, but the skillful and imaginative use of one might let you know you are reading the work of a talented person. A convention of spy movies, for example, is the high-speed chase. Once the chase begins, we know what is going on. We know every spy movie has to have this feature. We remember the many chases we have seen before, and we may even begin to anticipate some of the circumstances that must arise in this one: the upsetting of fruits and vegetables in a marketplace, the daring jump over some obstacle, the impossible squeeze between two eighteen-wheel trucks. We may also be bored: Here we go again. If the writer and director are clever and surprise us along the way, we will be delighted with the convention. The same applies in literature. Look for the conventions (the more you read, the more readily you will recognize them), and try to decide why and how the author is using them.

Archetypes

The archetype is also a pattern found in various literary works, but it is a different pattern from the convention. The archetype bears a deeper, more significant meaning. A high-speed automobile chase, while it might suggest something about the frenzy of modern life, usually is merely a device to increase suspense and entertainment in a film. To make something more of it—like a commentary on the frenzy of modern life—is to stretch its purpose. Such an observation is fairly trivial—that is, it only tells us something we already know. When literary critics talk of archetypes in literature, they are borrowing the term from depth psychology, and they mean patterns or recurring symbols that help us to know ourselves and all humanity with more perception. Archetypal patterns are to be found, of course, not only in Western literature but in various cultures throughout human history. These patterns capture the deepest and most significant experiences within human communities from very primitive times to our own day. One critic, Northrop Frye, says that an archetype is "a symbol which connects one poem with another and thereby helps to unify and integrate our literary experience."[12] When a story presents a character on a long and perilous journey, we may think of Ulysses or the people of Israel or the *Ancient Mariner* and the many other stories centered on such a journey. When a narrative tells of a sacrificial death, we may think of the Gospel accounts of Jesus and the countless attempts of writers to parallel or draw upon that event. Archetypes help us to make connections between the various stories we read and our own most important experiences.[13]

Setting

From the setting of a story we learn something of the conditions under which the characters live. By setting we mean the description of the historical time and geographical location of the story's action and the immediate surrounding of the events: everything from the furnishings of a room to the weather conditions. The setting may sometimes have a very dramatic effect on developments within the story (as when thunder and lightning accompany moments of high excitement or passion, perhaps in a gothic novel), or setting may subtly fill in background and round out impressions. The writer will, of course, use images to portray the setting, one element of fiction building on another. One critic suggests that we think of setting in terms of the atmosphere of a story, the conditions over which the characters have no control, conditions that define the limitations under which they live.[14]

Style

For most readers it may be harder to talk about style than about other elements of fiction. Style has to do with the way the words appear on the page, the way sentences are formed, the way metaphors and similes and images and allusions are put together within the work, the way the language is used, the kind and level of vocabulary. When we speak of style, we are speaking of the most personal and individualistic element of fiction. One critic has called style the "signature of the artist's will."[15] Perhaps for that reason it is more difficult to assess the contribution of an author's style to the reader's interpretive task. The author's style may seem to be more a matter of personal taste in reading material than something that can be objectively evaluated. Some people like Faulkner's long and involved sentences, for example; others prefer Hemingway's crisp and direct sentences. We can learn—taste aside—to evaluate at least some of the features of a writer's style. We can tell if we are bored with too many sentences of the same length and structure and with a weak vocabulary, and we can tell when the language is unnecessarily flowery and when it is much too mechanical. We will also be able to tell, as we make such judgments, when the style is really appropriate to the overall meaning of the narrative.

Tone

The tone of a story is also hard to pin down. When we listen to another person talk, we can determine a great deal about that person's intentions by facial expressions, gestures, the emphasis given to certain words, the softness or loudness of the voice. Usually we know whether a speaker is serious or playful or angry. With the written word, of course, judgments about tone are much more difficult. In discussing tone, we do more than ask if the writer is serious: we also try to catch those shades of meaning that enable us, to some extent, to read between the lines and know more than we are really being told. It is under the heading of tone, for example, that we can consider the use of irony in a work of fiction. Though we might always like to believe whatever we read and trust all the characters to be truthful with us, we know that literature, like life, is not like that. So we are forever testing the reading for accuracy and believability. "Irony" refers to the way a writer can say one thing on the page and really mean another. A character may speak sarcastically; a character may voice one opinion when we know from having heard her thoughts that she thinks another; the narrator may reveal things to the reader that the characters in the story do not yet know. The writer's attitude toward such mixtures of truth and deception adds tension and builds the tone of the work.

A reader is aware of tone also when the writer becomes humorous or playful. To understand the type of humor in a story is to focus on tone. Sometimes the reader will realize that the tone of a narrative has shifted: the second section of Alice Walker's "The Welcome Table" (see chapter 9) is a good example of a change of tone from a mixture of irony and moral purpose to playfulness. Most readers will need some practice asking about tone and analyzing it before they feel comfortable with this element of fiction. Tone is sometimes subtle, often complex, but when readers can recognize and name the tone or tones of a story they will have made progress toward grasping its purpose as well.

Theme

We consider the theme of a story last among these elements simply because each of the others contributes to this one. This is another entangled issue.[16] For our purposes here, I am only suggesting that readers might go beyond analysis of specific elements of a story (character, plot, style, and so forth) to some discussion of what the story ultimately conveys: what it or its author intends to communicate, what its ideas are, its conclusions or advice or philosophy. For some stories, we may not be able to answer such questions, or we may not want to; for others, we may begin to make some guesses. The process of discussing a story's theme has two steps: first, we decide if we can what the story's general topic is, and we try to capture that topic with a word or a phrase; next, we try to say what the story communicates about that topic, and here we might formulate a clause or a sentence. Perhaps the story is about human pride or the loss of innocence or some social issue. Perhaps its theme statement might expand the simple topic; we could suggest that the story says, for example, "The loss of innocence is a necessary, though painful, step toward maturity," or "The loss of innocence is society's cruel undermining of genuine and basic human instincts and values." This is no automatic operation, however, and we take these steps with caution.

It might be possible to read a certain story and go immediately to the question of what it means and make some determination about that rather quickly. It would be most possible to do so if the writer should oblige us by stating specifically a moral at the conclusion of the tale. Most contemporary writers do not make matters so simple for us, of course, and we need to consider many angles before we are ready to say what a story might mean. Our judgments about character and structure and symbols and allusions and all the rest are means of accumulating evidence toward some decision about the story's theme. We are cautious because the theme of a story is not likely to be reducible to one clear and unambiguous statement. For one thing, if the writer had only one simple statement to relate to us, he or she might well not bother with developing the complicated narrative; for another, several readers are not likely to agree on a single, simple statement of theme. When we try to say what a story is about, therefore, we are not looking for *one* meaning but for a rich and complex association of meanings coming to us through the variety of fictional elements.

A theme is inseparable from its story. Flannery O'Connor warned against trying to abstract some simple theme statement from a narrative; she said, "Some people have the notion that you read the story and then climb out of it into the meaning, but for the fiction writer himself the whole story is the meaning, because it is an experience, not an abstraction."[17] Using more picturesque language, she put it this way:

> People talk about the theme of a story as if the theme were like the string that a sack of chicken feed is tied with. They think that if you can pick out the theme, the way you pick the right thread in the chicken-feed sack, you can rip the story open and feed the chickens.[18]

She goes on to say that if you could separate the theme from a story in that fashion, the story would not be very good: "A story is a way to say something that can't be said any other way, and it takes every word in the story to say what the meaning is. You tell a story because a statement would be inadequate."[19] In part, meaning comes to us as we enter the world of the story, read carefully, and concentrate on the many dimensions of the narrative. Even then, we may have to settle for ambiguity or for several possibilities of significance.

THE BACKGROUND OF THE TEXT

Although the text itself is the basic unit for the reader's attention, sometimes there is benefit in looking also beyond the text. The value of this examination will vary, of course, from story to story. We need not spend much time on this technique; but since it may be important for some stories, we should note that investigation of the background of a text may be a useful tool for the interpreter. In analyzing background, we might want to know the time and cultural situation under which the story was written, as an aid to comprehending some of the things taking place in the narrative. If we read Faulkner's *Intruder in the Dust*,[20] for example, we read more intelligently if we recall (or search out, if it is not in our memories) the racial climate in the South during the 1940s and 1950s; and if we then read Madison Jones's *A Cry of Absence*,[21] we need to recall the racial climate of the South in the 1960s. These two very different stories arise in different historical circumstances, even in different communities (Mississippi and Alabama towns), and knowledge of the background helps us sharpen those differences in our minds and observe some similarities.

We may also want to know, in dealing with the background of a narrative, the type of story it is. If we are reading a tall tale, for instance—the stories of Paul Bunyan or, in Southern literature, tales of the old Southwest[22]—we profit from being aware of that particular form of narrative, where and how it developed, what some of the other stories of that type have been, and what its rules and conventions are. Since the tall tale frequently depends on exaggeration, regional dialect, buffoon heroes, and comic situations, our evaluation of a story that seems to fall into this category will depend to some degree on how well the story carries out the usual features of the form. The same would be true about science fiction stories or gothic tales or fantasies: we are better interpreters when we can place the story with other stories of its kind and let them help us understand and evaluate.

Still another part of the background we might want for interpreting a story is some consideration of what other readers have felt about it. In a sense, this may be part of analysis of the text if we assume that the other readers have also talked about such things as character development, style, and theme; but published criticism really does amount to material outside and beyond the text itself. In some cases, such material may not be available to you—though if you have time to do extra work on a story, it will be easy to examine, at your public library, a number of guides that will lead you to reviews of a book or essays of interpretation. This study will not spoil your own assessment of a story, but it will put you in touch with other interpreters and may lead you to some ideas you had not yet explored.

Tracking down allusions also leads outside the text and becomes part of the background analysis. When a character in a story is associated with Prometheus, for instance, and you don't recall that story, you need to consult an encyclopedia or index to mythology if you are to fill in the content implied by that association. That is reading beyond the text and is part of the background of the text. This illustrates why, for some readers some of the time, reading of the text alone is not enough. When the text leads us beyond itself, we have to follow it and do some secondary investigation if we are to appreciate what the text itself means.

THE AUTHOR

The author's life history and other achievements might also be considered part of the background of a text; but I am noting the author's role as a category separate from the textual background because the interpreter faces some particular problems in evaluating the relationship between the story and its writer. When we have read numerous stories by one writer, we are more comfortable with the writer's style and ideas and characters, and we may enter the writer's created world more easily. The caution we must exercise in building any connections between two different stories by a single author is simply that they are different works, written at different periods of time with distinct purposes. Even when the same character appears in two separate stories, we cannot assume that the character has the same ideas or values in both stories: in fact, the more realistic the creation of the character, the more likely the character has changed from one writing to the next. As Faulkner said when he was criticized for the inconsistencies within his characters who had appeared in both *The Hamlet* and *The Mansion*, a writer just might get to know characters better across the years. In a note which serves as a brief foreword to *The Mansion*, he advises the reader

> that the author has already found more discrepancies and contradictions than he hopes the reader will—contradictions and discrepancies due to the fact that the author has learned, he believes, more about the human heart and its dilemma than he knew thirty-four years ago; and is sure that, having lived with them that long time, he knows the characters in this chronicle better than he did then.[23]

In much the same way, the interpreter will beware of assuming that the story should be interpreted in terms of the writer's ideas as expressed elsewhere, either in other fiction or in any essay or interview. In this sense, again, the work of fiction has to stand on its own. Some critics make the mistake of assuming that the writer always means the same thing every time he or she speaks or writes: these critics make that mistake because they fail to enter the fictional world of the writer. Although a writer may speak through a character, we cannot automatically identify the character's voice with the author's; on the basis of such an assumption, there have been some strange misinterpretations of fiction. The key to avoiding this sort of error, of course, is to pay close attention to the text itself and to operate on the basis of the character's individuality and distinct development. Some critics are convinced that Gavin Stevens, the lawyer who appears in a number of Faulkner's novels and stories, is always speaking for Faulkner. Close observation of the stories and of Faulkner's nonfiction, however, suggests that, even though Stevens and Faulkner may agree about some human values, Stevens is quite a separate personality and cannot simply be reduced to the role of author's mouthpiece.

Maybe the thorniest issue of all in the author-text relationship is the question of the author's intention. Can we know what the author really means to communicate in a work of fiction? And if so, how? Critical opinion is, as we might suspect, mixed.[24] Some critics warn us of the mistake of assuming that we can know what the author means to convey in the story: after all, an author may have a change of mind or may not be able to find the right words and images to deliver those intentions within the story. Others argue that by reading carefully we can uncover or reconstruct what the author means: after all, the author uses all those fictional elements, and puts them together in some fashion that must have purpose; as we examine the text and ask questions and probe the common meanings of words and allusions, we come close to what the author wanted us to get.

My own suggestion is that we proceed slowly and recognize the difficulty of this part of interpretation. It does not matter, in the long run, if we remain somewhat tentative in our conclusions about the author's intention and focus more on what we understand the text to say (supporting that with clear references to the text). We may well be quite close to what the author meant when we follow through with an analysis of the elements of fiction, and not much is to be gained by bold pronouncements that we have recovered unambiguously the meaning of a story just as the author wanted us to.

How are we to proceed, then, when the author tells us somewhere else exactly what a particular story should mean? Though it is often exciting to get such authorial assistance in our interpreting, we might do better to insist that the work itself bear out the author's interpretation. Some writers—Faulkner, for instance (as a general rule)—refuse to offer interpretations of their own stories, claiming not to remember a story or being unwilling to intrude on the reader's job. Even when a writer tells us—as Flannery O'Connor sometimes does—just what the clues to meaning are, we still have to be careful. I want to examine the story, and if I can't find her "intended" meaning within the text, I'm inclined to trust the text and concede that she may have failed to get across what she wanted to convey.

That leads to another issue: trusting and not trusting the author. On the one hand, it is fair to assume that when a writer goes to all the trouble to write out a story, fussing over words and phrases, writing and rewriting, he or she knows what is happening and makes decisions about the text thoughtfully and purposefully. When a good writer names a character Joe Christmas or Obadiah Elihue Parker, there was most likely reason to do so. Whether we can determine that reason is another matter: we cannot be satisfied with the most apparent and straightforward reason, since the writer may be making an ironic suggestion by a name. On the one hand, we can trust that a writer consciously and skillfully builds a work of fiction; our job is to examine the finished product and see how the pieces fit together. On the other hand, however, sometimes even good writers make mistakes, and bad ones do so more often. When, in a story, we come to a passage that does not make sense—a place where a character seems to be out of the role or where action seems unmotivated—we owe the writer our most deliberate study to make sure we are not just missing something. But if we cannot solve the problem, and if other readers confirm the difficulty, we should not give in and think ourselves stupid. Writers do make mistakes, and the good critic can spot those errors and try to figure out why they happened.

What we hope for in writers is that they will enable us to see things we have never seen before and that they will direct us toward the truthfulness of the varied realities of our lives. They are not really preachers—we can't expect that—but they open to us the created order with imagination and sensitivity. If they try to preach, they may become propagandists, and the story will be incidental to its message; perhaps the story will be no longer true, no longer an accurate, believable reflection of our common experiences (I will say more about the relationship between truth and storytelling in chapter 4). What we hope is that the writer will lead us into a story so that the new story before us fits and interprets the old stories of our lives. To make a story true, the author must be a word mistress, an image builder, a sentence crafter, an illusion popper, an observer, a namer, a prophet. Confined and rebellious as we are, the writer cannot save us; but he or she can awaken us.

THE READER

In some critical circles, it has been held that the reader was rather inconsequential to the whole interpretive task.[25] After all, the work itself is quite objective: there are the words on the page. Even the background could be considered objective: history, biography, sociology, facts. When we come to the reader, however, we reach the subjective territory that is so uncertain, so slippery. Each reader brings a different set of experiences to any piece of fiction, and each reader, therefore, may interpret each work as he or she wishes—and we would be left with a thousand different readings and be no better off than before we started. What we need is objectivity, something we can count on, something plain and indisputable; so we turn back to the text. Nevertheless, we understand that there can be no pushing aside of the reader. A story is written to be read, and the writer knows what risks are being unfolded and what possibilities for misreading there will inevitably be with any work presented to a large and varied—and perhaps undiscriminating—audience. We cannot overlook the place of each reader's experience in the interpretative task: we go on to ask how we can navigate around subjective misreadings and toward some commonly accepted standards upon which a number of readers might agree.

First, credit must be given where it is due: without the reader, the story rests in all its glorious objectivity, amusing no one and doing no one any good. Maybe writers a century or more ago realized that more clearly than some do today. Readers may take heart: they are one of the keys to interpretation. They too have imagination and rational responsibilities, an assignment to read well, imagine freely, and advance into a new world even if they must leave it in fifteen minutes to go back to earning their living or caring for their family. Take your own experiences and beliefs and judgments about literature seriously—but not too seriously; remember to have some fun as well. Don't let your own prejudices worry you overmuch. Other readers have their prejudices as well; there is no such thing as an unbiased reader. The trick is to balance those presuppositions and prejudices against some measurements that you know are external to you: remember the various elements of fiction that need to be evaluated; recall the questions you might ask to get a broad and inclusive reading; and check your own conclusions with other readers as an important hedge against entirely subjective interpretation.

Reading is an active vocation. Some readers of our day seem to expect literature to entertain them with the same intensity as a television program. As we grow more accustomed to the total impact of the visual media, we may decide that reading is a rather dull pastime. Or it may be that in watching a television program we can shift our imaginations into neutral and let the screen provide all the images and do all the thinking. (We cannot really do that with television, I believe: although a series of dull-witted shows and commercials may have a mind-numbing effect on us, a well-produced program will engage our senses and can offer many of the same benefits literature offers.) Perhaps we need to cultivate an attitude of active reading, reading that is mature and sensitive, with the reader totally involved in the fiction. The reader cannot expect, from even the best literature, that the words will jump off the page and direct every thought and feeling. Active reading means reading with a mind and imagination alert to the multitude of potentials resting among the words on the page. Some people complain that baseball is a slow and boring game and would like to see it tightened up and shortened the way some readers would enjoy a Faulkner story more if it were only a few pages long. A true baseball fan, however, watches a game actively and can never be a mere spectator: he or she thinks about each pitch, wondering whether the pitcher will throw a fastball, curve, or sinker, wondering what the batter is expecting, guessing about the manager's strategy. If you don't know and love the game, you may think all this talk is foolishness. A reader is engaged in the reading—anticipating, unraveling, imagining, with each new sentence and phrase. That is part of the delight.

The questions the reader will ask may be fairly obvious by now, but some of them take on a slightly new dimension when we approach them from the standpoint of the reader and not so much that of the author or text. From the reader's viewpoint, the reason to ask about the meaning of an allusion is not simply to get a dictionary or encyclopedia definition but to see also how the allusion might have entered that reader's life at some point. The reason to check the meanings of words is not just to see how the author is using them but to see if the reader has a firm grasp of the definitions and what special connotations those words might have in the reader's vocabulary. We examine a symbol not with total objectivity—impossible!—but to see how that symbol affects us. We study a character to see if we might discover ourselves somewhere in that person's quirks and graces. We read the story not so we can outline its plot and structure and make a chronology of the events but to see how the story of our own lives is repeated and ennobled there. That we are studying those precise, observable elements of fiction is our safeguard against undue subjectivism; that we are studying them within the context of our own experiences is our safeguard against a pointless objectivism.

More remains to be said about the role of the reader in the task of interpretation. This book is meant to help the reader perform critical skills so that literature can be most beneficial. For the moment it should be clear that the interpreter has a perplexing, demanding job. How do our imaginations handle the discoveries we make? How do we engage other people in dialogue about them and get some correction and support from a larger community? What happens when we confront a specific story? Before we can move on to these last two questions, we need to think together about how we actually evaluate a work of literature, how we apply our developing critical dexterity to decisions about the value of particular stories.

4

EVALUATING

In some ways, evaluation is inseparable from the task of analysis we have been describing: to analyze is to evaluate. Yet we are often inclined to make some decision about whether a given story is good or bad. We do this to bring our reading to a conclusion, to pass some judgment, wrap the matter up neatly, and move on to something else. I'm not always sure just why we need to make evaluations with the precision and finality that usually seem to be expected. Perhaps "Please rank this on a scale of one to ten" has become a rule for many of our experiences. Some people would be happier to say simply, "I liked it" or "I didn't like it" and "Now leave me alone." Once again, I propose a middle ground: let's avoid feeling that we must come to indelible decisions about the value of a work of art; but let's also try to be able to say, without too much bother, why we like a particular book or story.

To face one extreme, we can note difficulties of placing narratives in absolute categories. Above all, categories like positive and negative, religious and nonreligious, Christian and non-Christian have very limited usefulness. As was noted in chapter 2, the meaning of the terms has to be specified clearly, and different readers will not agree about how to do that. Readers' judgments are also inevitably different, so a discussion about whether to consider a story positive or negative may go on forever and get nowhere, since each reader will understand not only the categories but also the story itself according to a personal standard of judgment. That is, if the point of discussion is placing the story in a category, the result may prove fruitless. If, on the other hand, we keep asking *why* we make certain judgments, we may come closer to a helpful kind of evaluation.

The other extreme ("just let me read; don't ask me questions") may be the course many readers would prefer and—let's acknowledge it—

should sometimes take. As we have already observed, a great deal can be said for literature as escape and entertainment, and we need not feel a compulsion always to analyze and fret over things we have enjoyed. Some books, of course, will not leave us alone: you put them back on the shelf, but the characters and their situations remain with you for days, gnawing at you and calling for reflection. Other books you can read, become absorbed in, have a pleasant experience from, and then put away with scarcely another thought. Thank God for both kinds. Obviously, if you agree to read a book with other people, you are committed to some level of evaluation: one purpose of the group will have been to discuss the reading, and you will hardly be able to sit back in the corner and plead that you don't want to be disturbed.

So the question now is how we evaluate a work of literature. What are some of the legitimate steps we might take? What sorts of questions should we ask? What standards can we apply? What special problems will we face? How can we enjoy what we're doing and feel relatively relaxed about it? In dealing with these questions, we are not so much trying to decide whether a particular story is three-star or four-star; rather, we are reaching for some clarity about what we mean when we say, "Now, that was really a good book!" It does make sense that we should be able to say why we enjoyed a story. It especially makes sense when we read with a group or talk about our reading with someone over lunch or coffee: we evaluate not just to complete a mechanical process but for the sake of one another and our mutual understanding. I say why for your sake, and you say why for mine.

THE LITERARY STANDARD

At one level—to return to the starting point of the present chapter—to analyze is to evaluate. To make that equation is to say that, as we examine the background of the narrative, the author's role, our own impressions, and the various elements of the text, we are forming judgments about the story. In chapter 3 we discussed those standards; now look back at a few of them to see how analysis relates to evaluation. If we read a story where the author's "intention" is plainly exposed, we will recognize that the story has lost a great deal of subtlety and doesn't really stimulate our minds, except perhaps as propaganda. Or if we read a story filled with flat characters, we may decide the author has not presented believable personalities. Or if we read a story where there seem to be no allusions, the images are commonplace, and the language largely abstract, then we may find our imaginations stimulated only to a minimum. At each point of our investigation of the story, in other words, we are looking to see how the writer has performed, how the story works. The better those technical features of the fiction have been handled, the higher our total evaluation. We will see in a moment that other questions must also be raised and that a technically precise story may not always be the best story; still, we carry out a major part of evaluation when we make literary judgments.

Basic to evaluation, then, is the literary standard. Other standards may appeal to us at various moments in our own histories and in certain books. Many readers are inclined to build a groundwork for evaluation resting on an abiding interest of their own: political, sociological, scientific, or religious. Though such areas may be important for us to consider as we read any book, we move away from literary evaluation as we judge the book purely in terms of its uniformity with a political, sociological, scientific, or religious viewpoint. With some stories we can determine, to be sure, whether they espouse democratic capitalism or a form of socialism. If we are democratic capitalists and reject a book solely because it advocates socialism, we have not made a literary judgment. We are perfectly free to make those determinations, but we should be clear that we are not, in such a case, using literary standards. A story that seems to favor socialism may turn out to be better—in its development of character, power of allusion and symbol, consistency of theme and point of view, for example—than a story that seems to favor democratic capitalism. The reverse could be true as well. We can ask any questions we wish of a narrative, but the literary standard remains the basic one for evaluation.

If we say that the literary standard is basic to evaluation, we have not, of course, solved all our problems. We still have to know exactly what we mean by a "literary standard" and what presuppositions exist behind our use of the term. Here, once again, we are on slippery turf. To be sure, I have implied certain judgments as I have listed the various elements of fiction and as I have talked about applying a literary standard. I have made positive mention of stimulated imaginations, vivid language, subtlety, and believable characters. Who is to say that these are superior traits of literature? Maybe you like flat characters, understand them better, and get more from their stories. Who is to tell you that a story with only flat characters is often an inferior story? Clearly, one way to answer that question is to bow to individual taste and abdicate critical judgment altogether: if we were willing to do that, we would have little basis for this or any other discussion of fiction. We can acknowledge that not all readers have had the same experiences in reading or in life; we can allow flexibility in our literary decisions; we can avoid judging other readers on the basis of their sophistication or lack thereof. We need not always agree which criteria are primary, but we can work with a list of feasible criteria and test those in our reading together. You may not be completely satisfied with the ones I present: their own validity will appear as you read fiction, and apply them, and eventually determine whether they or some others help you make decisions and explain your responses to the literature you read.

Response to the literature is, after all, what we are interested in here. We are not discussing evaluation in some abstract way. We are instead trying to spell out as carefully as possible why certain stories appeal to us and how we can discuss that appeal intelligently with one another, representing both our own subjective assessments and the more objective characteristics that appear in the text. We are asking how we find literature that excites us, prods us, engages our attention, pleases, encourages, and benefits. What is it about a story that causes it to do these things? If literature has value for us, we can communicate that value to one another more precisely, more helpfully, as we operate from some accurately stated standards of measurement that are, at the same time, not entirely circumscribed. We cannot be impartial readers; neither can we be indifferent.

Although technical excellence is one of the features we expect to find in good literature, another would certainly be the literature's bearing of its appropriate benefits. We have discussed what those benefits might be and have recognized that a good story might entertain us, help us understand ourselves and our world a little better, and present human values for our reflection. If those are indeed among literature's benefits, we might evaluate a piece of fiction by the extent to which it does those things; a truly good story might well do all four. If we come upon a narrative which accomplishes none of the four, we would be justified in dismissing it as inferior. Could it be that a story might express these benefits and be a technical disaster? Could you enjoy a story and feel enriched by it and at the same time decide that it was poorly written and consistently weak in its expression of the major elements of fiction? That might be possible, though I am strongly inclined to doubt it. Experience generally shows that when a story brings benefits, it does so precisely because it is skillfully told. You will have to see if, in your own reading, you find such a parallel between an expression of benefits and technical excellence.[1]

SOME QUESTIONS TO ASK
OF A STORY

In addition to asking yourself if a story is well written and if it presents clear advantages for its readers, you might raise a number of other issues. No one of these will be sufficient for the task of evaluation, and it will not be necessary in every instance to raise all of these questions. I list them here in the hope of providing some concrete examples of how you might estimate the value of your reading. Other questions may also come to your mind. If you are reading with a group, you would do well to agree on some standards of evaluation before you begin; these standards do not have to be unchangeable, but some clarity about common assumptions and evaluative questions should prove helpful.

Is It True?

One thing you will want to determine is whether or not the story—its characters, situation, language—can be believed. Do you feel as though the people of the story are real people? Do they exhibit emotions and fears and hopes similar to your own or those of other people you have known? Are their motivations for action clear and believable? Can you imagine a real human being doing those things, thinking those thoughts, saying those words? This standard is not without limitations, of course, since readers may disagree about what is realistic. Still, asking the questions will lead you into those points of disagreement if they do exist.

Even a realistic story may turn out not to be believable to some readers. Critics often describe the fiction of the late nineteenth century and early twentieth century as "realistic" fiction, meaning that for the first time writers provided more vivid details of actual life experience, were more candid in their description of human emotions, thoughts, and actions, and were less inclined to be flowery or romantic in their portrayal of a person's story. Writers began to use dialect in order to capture the actual speech of the people of a certain region; some attempted to make the reader see the peculiar sights of a particular place (local color); others broached subjects, such as infidelity and divorce, that had been forbidden a generation earlier. "Realistic" fiction is true-to-life; it hides nothing, tells all. Whether such fiction is believable depends a great deal on the reader, of course. A reader who has been raised on a farm in the southern United States, has been an active church-goer, and has never spent more than a few days in any city larger than one hundred thousand inhabitants may have a hard time believing a story about black people trapped in a northern ghetto, or immigrants working in factories, or corruption in big business. Such a reader may be quite honest in saying, "I don't know anyone like that; I've never experienced anything like that." And no matter how accurately the story had portrayed those circumstances, the story would not seem true to this particular reader. Not all readers will agree about what constitutes realism, and the most vivid details will not always be believable.

At the same time, a story may be quite believable and realistic even if it is fantasy or is written in or about an age very different from our own. When we read a work of science fiction, or one of C. S. Lewis's Narnia tales, or even a short story by Hawthorne or a play by Shakespeare, we find episodes and characters that clearly do not belong in our world. Yet we understand that the ideas behind these stories have a validity of their own. In the science fiction or fantasy, we recognize that the writer is using these unfamiliar words to express attitudes about our own world. The fantastic becomes a device that might give us some distance from our own situations and lead us— despite the distance or because of it—to see some truth about ourselves. In some other contemporary literature, such as Walker Percy's *The Second Coming*,[2] for instance, we may not always be sure what is happening in the story, since some sequences occur within a character's imagination or dreams, and we may find reality blurred. Yet the unclear or unbelievable features of the story may be the very things to convince us of deeper levels of reality. In the literature of other time periods, we frequently sense that what the writer is describing about the characters or events of that time is not at all bound to one period of history. We might say there is something universal about the theme of the older story, that it deals with a truth applicable in all times for all people. Thus "universality" becomes an important trait of good and lasting literature. As we seek the truth of literature, the search remains broad and goes far beyond simple identity with observable facts. Indeed, a close parallel with concrete reality does not guarantee truthfulness: a most realistic story, filled with graphic details and accurate descriptions, may turn out to offer a false interpretation, a dangerous philosophy. A science fiction story may have, for example, quite credible presentations of scientific technology and may realistically describe outer space and interplanetary travel but may set forth a dehumanizing philosophy.

In making all these distinctions, of course, we are really raising the old philosophical questions about the meaning of truth. Truth clearly does not mean, in the sense we are using it here, simply a conformity to what actually exists or what a person might actually experience. When a writer sets a story in a town that cannot be located on a map, we do not immediately dismiss the town as unrealistic and unbelievable; rather, we look for other signs of its realism in the way the town and its inhabitants are described. William Faulkner named the major town of his stories Jefferson, Mississippi, and located it in the northwestern corner of that state. There was no town named Jefferson in those parts, but readers familiar with the territory could note striking parallels between Faulkner's Jefferson and his actual place of residence, Oxford, Mississippi. Local people in Oxford now like to point out the sites of their town and tell you in which of Faulkner's stories they appear—though there was a day when they resented his use of their town in his fiction and feared that his portrait of local residents might be too close to home. It is fine if someone thinks a house in a story is modeled after my house, but please don't think the cowardly miser who lives there bears any resemblance to me! Ah, truth!

The Romantic poet and essayist Samuel Taylor Coleridge has provided one of the classic phrases for this discussion: he said we read literature making a "willing suspension of disbelief."[3] That is to say, when we pick up a story, we know it may carry us into new territory, and we submit to the author's vision of reality. We are, therefore, agreeable to accepting some things—coincidence perhaps, or fantasy, or distant time periods—and we manage to believe that the truth of the literary work is not impaired by the unreality we seem to be experiencing in those pages as we read. Therefore, when we ask if a story is true, we are not expecting it to be totally realistic on all counts, and we are not really measuring its truthfulness by our usual standards; rather, we are measuring truthfulness, in a deeper sense, by the way the work squares generally with our experience. In Anne Tyler's *Dinner at the Homesick Restaurant*,[4] when Pearl Tull refuses to acknowledge to her children that their father has left his family and will never return, the reader may feel that Mrs. Tull's reaction is not really the way anyone would handle even so painful an abandonment. As we ask about whether this account is true, however, we are not just asking if it is likely that we would do such a thing or that anyone we know would; we are asking if this character in this particular story, given her life history, her own personality, would do such a thing. If the author gives us enough background and makes clear the character's motivation—as, I submit, Tyler does here—then we can believe the story despite our misgivings about the working out of this segment. We suspend our tendency to disbelieve for a moment so that we can attempt to see a larger truth to which the author is pointing.

Pursuing that matter of a larger truth, we run into further difficulties. When we ask if a story is true, are we also asking about its agreement with our own philosophical or theological persuasions? What I have said so far in this section does not carry the question of a story's truthfulness into such depths; but, of course, any reader may want to raise the larger issue. We need to recognize a distinction, however. In this sense, "Is it true?" means "Does it agree with my world view?" or "Do I share its world view?" and that becomes a risky evaluative question. We can certainly ask it, but when we do, we are beginning to move beyond mere evaluation of the story as a piece of literature. Here is an issue we have already discussed: a story that presents a world view similar to my own may be a bad story by all literary standards, and a story with a very different world view may be beautifully written, imaginatively conceived, and so may qualify as excellent literature. We can ask about its basic truthfulness to our own theological position, but let's be clear that the answer to this question will not settle the literary value of the story under examination.[5]

Is It Complicated?

We may like to understand what we are reading, but we sometimes come across stories that are too easy—so easy that they never make us wonder or experience anything exciting or profound. The complication of a story is related to its truthfulness. We may realize that life as we experience it is never really very simple; we may wish for clear, self-evident explanations of what happens around us, but we rarely find that easy explanations hold up to actual causes and effects. When a human relationship is destroyed, for example, as we hear the story we find a multitude of reasons. What one party expresses may well conflict with the impressions of the other, and observers of the breakup might have altogether different judgments. If the truth of that situation is to be found—and perhaps it cannot be—we need as full an account as possible, just as investigators of an automobile accident need testimony from as many witnesses as possible.

The complexity of a story is related to its perspectives. I discussed in the last chapter the importance of analyzing a narrative's point of view, and I mentioned Faulkner's use of multiple narrators in his novel *Absalom, Absalom!* One of Faulkner's favorite storytellers, the sewing machine salesman V. K. Ratliff, seems to thrive on ferreting out the multitude of details that might explain human experience, that might help someone get at the whole story. Ratliff accuses his lawyer friend, Gavin Stevens, of misunderstanding what is happening because he, like all lawyers (according to Ratliff), wants to make matters too complicated: "He's a lawyer, and to a lawyer, if it aint complicated it dont matter whether it works or not because if it aint complicated up enough it aint right and so even if it works, you dont believe it."[6] What Ratliff says may well apply to Faulkner's fiction and, in some sense, to all good literature: "if it aint complicated up enough it aint right." Complications and ambiguities help make a story realistic and believable.

A story is complicated when it is inclusive.[7] If a narrative describes with precision and accuracy the world in which we live—say, we find a novel set in our own home town at the time of our childhood—we may enjoy that story with a certain nostalgia. We will have ways of testing the descriptive powers of the authors, and we may well recognize ourselves and some of our actual experiences within the fictional account. No one need dispute the enjoyment or other value of such reading. Still, literature that takes us beyond our own experience and introduces us to other people with other problems will challenge us and broaden us and will have fulfilled its potential for benefit, even though it may be difficult for us to grasp at first reading everything that goes on in the story. A literary work may be narrow and provincial when it is confined to one time and region; it may be sentimental when it is confined to one range of emotions. An inclusive literature will introduce the reader to opinions and feelings, as well as people and places, that are not altogether comprehended and shared. Those unknown dimensions of a work may make it not only more complicated and ambiguous but richer as well.

Some readers have trouble with ambiguous narratives; yet many critics would suggest that ambiguity is one of the marks of good fiction. To be sure, life itself is ambiguous, but isn't it some relief to read a story that takes us away from the confusion and unsettlement of our own lives and lets us at least imagine a situation where problems are easily solved and dreams happily fulfilled? Sometimes this is exactly the kind of reading we want. Yet at other times we may wish for something more true to our own experience, since only literature that accurately reflects our lives can help us muddle through the turmoil, gain some perspective, and live together with more wisdom and purpose. The story that wraps everything up neatly, where all the characters solve all their problems and live happily ever after, will not only prove unrealistic, it will finally bore us, since there will be little suspense, little conflict, and therefore little to anticipate. Ambiguity in a story serves to deepen our sense of reality, to hold us in suspense, to engage our minds and emotions.

But what if a story is so ambiguous that we do not even understand it? When we say something like this, we may mean that the story is obscure to us rather than ambiguous, or that it is so complex as to be obscure. A story may well *be* obscure, of course: its characters can be poorly drawn, its language abstract, its plot either too convoluted or too empty. If we have done a thorough analysis and have found these features of the fiction to be inadequately developed, then we will have discovered a reason for the obscurity and will be justified in passing some negative judgment on the work itself. Complexity for its own sake is no virtue. Sometimes, when a story seems too obscure or too ambiguous, that can be our fault as readers more than the author's fault; sometimes, as we reread, we find we have simply missed meanings that are really there in the text. We may have read carelessly (though we do not like to admit it), and we may not have done the analysis necessary to the comprehension of well-developed literature. If you read and do not grasp what you are reading, you may need to read again. The necessity of a second reading is not a poor reflection of your reading ability, nor is it always a judgment against the writer. A serious, penetrating story may require several readings if you are to reach its depth, catch its nuances, and receive its greatest benefits. When you read the second or third time, you will be alert to subtle shadings of characterization, to allusions and symbols, to intricacies of plot and point of view. The second time around, you may be able to look for answers to the puzzles you found in the first reading, and you may go a little more slowly at spots where you had been confused. You can try to be certain that all the pronoun references are absolutely clear to you and that you are aware of the author's use of irony; each of these represents an element of a narrative that may be confusing to a reader. A good book, a well-written story, will repay your efforts many times over.

Is It New?

Still another question that may be raised about fiction has to do with its freshness, its ability to surprise and evoke a new awareness of reality. Here, as elsewhere, the standard of evaluation is clearly affected by the reader's own personal reading background. Even without broad reading experience, however, many readers will recognize that some of the words on the page are trite and all too familiar. They will know when material is too much like what they have read before, and they will know when it is simply a replay of ordinary events of life. What we look for in literature is a new perspective, a fresh approach so that we can have ways of judging our ordinary experiences, ways of understanding ourselves and our world from new angles, something to lift us out of our ruts.

Stories can surprise us in many ways. They may present some new and interesting personalities with whom we have not been acquainted in our own lives; they may carry us through a tragedy or joy we have not known; they may take us to new worlds, parts of the globe we have never visited, or lands of fantasy we have never imagined could exist. They may surprise us with unexpected twists of plot. We may think we know how a character will act in certain circumstances, only to find that we have been fooled, that there are dimensions of the character we had not yet realized. If the characters' actions are indeed clearly motivated within the story, we can review the steps of the narrative and realize that the author has really prepared us in artful ways for what was to happen. Our surprise may come because the development has been carried out with such expertise. We might say that the more realistic a story is, the more surprises it will have for us: life itself constantly confronts us with the unexpected. The wording of a tale can form another medium of freshness, as the writer gives descriptions in language we find new and exciting. Where the language is trivial and commonplace, we will not be engaged in the story, and we may rightly judge the narrative to be inferior.

Are the Elements of the Story Appropriate to One Another?

Under the heading of appropriateness, a number of questions will occur to the reader. A basic issue has to do with whether the form of the story is appropriate to its content. A narrative about suffering and death may not work very well unless the style is serious; a story about children at play may not be effective if the writer seems altogether too somber; a tall tale is proper form for some topics but not for others. Tragedy requires dignity and gravity. You will readily sense when the form and content do not seem to belong together. If, from everything that goes on in the story, you feel the author means to elevate the subject of the narrative, yet the language is frivolous and lighthearted, the plot trivial, the characters insincere, you will recognize that something is wrong. You could have been mistaken about the intention, but it may also be that the writer has failed to match form and content. Other levels of inappropriateness may also lead you to such a conclusion. The speech of the characters should be true to the speech patterns of their region and class; the degree and type of irony should match the theme of the story; the allusions should be fitting to the time and place of the narrative. If something seems out of line in the story you are reading, double-check to make sure you have read correctly and that your assumptions of the author's purposes are accurate. Where you find glaring inconsistencies, you must acknowledge weakness in the text.

This is not to imply that there can never be any inconsistencies. One can have a humorous tale about a serious subject or elevated language about a lowlife setting. Look for consistency within the work itself. Faulkner's story of Addie Bundren's death and burial (*As I Lay Dying*)[8] is at once serious and comical. The narrative contains clear passages to let the reader know of the pain and conflict within the lives of the characters; yet the delightfully funny sequences and dialogue relieve the intensity of the story and help provide a context from which the tragedy can be understood, or at least faced. In much of Faulkner's fiction, characters will speak in dialect but think in elegant Faulknerian prose. That may seem inconsistent, but Faulkner's prose style becomes a means of presenting, for example, a child's reflections, unlimited by the child's age or vocabulary and thus finally more expressive of what the child actually feels. Faulkner is using the language the child would have used had it been available to him or her—all so that the character might more realistically be portrayed and the reader have a sharper sense of the narrative. For a child of eight from rural Mississippi to speak in elaborately constructed sentences and advanced vocabulary would be inconsistent; for that child to think in such language is not necessarily inconsistent if we accept the device of the author as necessary within a particular narrative.

Does the Story Come to You with an Established Reputation, or Does It Compare Well with Stories That Do?

Much of what we read has already been evaluated by someone, and we have little choice but to take those judgments with some earnestness. Certain stories will have earned a reputation over the years, maybe over centuries, and if they do not at first appeal to us, we do well to honor their past and read them more carefully. Shakespeare has been read and performed through many generations; if we have difficulty reading him today, we must at least ask what about his work has made its appeal so lasting. Usually we find that the work itself pays its own dividends and that its reputation is not simply the result of enthusiastic public relations efforts down through the years.

The accepted works of literature can become, in other words, touchstones for evaluation of contemporary fiction. We can recall the accomplishments of the great literature of the past and see how current writings compare with them in the various areas of judgment we have already discussed. This is not an infallible measurement, but then, none of the questions we have raised has been intended as an absolute mark to be applied in final and unthinking ways. Recognizing that we will not all agree on which pieces of world literature are to be considered touchstones, we can nonetheless use the best of the past to help us evaluate what we are presently reading. When we are reading, for instance, a story by a writer of our own day, a writer whose reputation is not yet secure, we can ask questions such as these: Will this story last beyond our generation? Why? Does this story have characteristics that will enable readers of another culture or period of history to benefit from it? Does the story approach the standards of theme and characterization and style that have been set by those people acknowledged as the great writers of our literature? This form of measurement can be hard on a writer, of course, since the writer may well suffer from the comparison. Flannery O'Connor once noted the difficulty Southern writers face in being compared to William Faulkner; she said, "Nobody wants his mule and wagon stalled on the same track the Dixie Limited is roaring down."[9] We do not want mere imitation from our writers, of course; that would be terribly dull. We can, however, use the comparison measurement, with some charity, to make our own determinations about new writers. We don't want everyone to be a Faulkner or an O'Connor, but we can hope for something of their power in storytelling, something of their humor and style, something of their deep humanity.

SOME PROBLEMS IN EVALUATION

Even when we read carefully and ask questions such as those I have suggested, we will continue to run into thorny problems. Suppose, for example, that one of the purposes of your reading is to get a feeling for your own times; your evaluation of a story will be determined in part by how well it provides that feeling and by how accurate you judge the author's description and analysis to be. In any case, it makes sense to move slowly and beware of the bold pronouncements.

After all, a vast body of literature has been produced, and no one person can possibly read every novel and short story that rolls off the presses. Even if you managed such a feat—you would have to be, at the very least, independently wealthy and a speed reader—you could still wind up misreading and so make a false analysis of the times. One critic has admitted reading such writers as Faulkner and Hemingway entirely negatively, seeing them as prophets of despair and so concluding that the whole culture was sunk in gloom; but as he came back to those writers another day, he found in them both humor and a positive emphasis.[10]

So much goes into the analysis of literature. A writer like Faulkner produces a story that seems best and most true, and readers don't rush to buy it; so he thinks about the kinds of books that sell and decides people want to read about sex and violence.[11] Then he writes a book full of sex and violence, and it makes his reputation. Critics read that book and either don't read or don't really understand Faulkner's other stories, and they pronounce him a prophet of negative philosophy. Reviews, at least sometimes, are written all too hastily and may well turn readers against a writer who is really pretty good. Or the culture prescribes what will sell and what won't. The writer of best sellers may furnish a more authentic index to the times than another writer who is trying hard to portray genuine human experiences. It isn't that we can't read our culture through our writers—to some extent we can—but we do well to use caution in drawing those conclusions and to recognize that the last word on contemporary writers comes in very slowly. Rather than asking what a particular novel says about our country or culture, we might ask what the characters in that novel are like, what the issues are, and if those characters and issues are to be found anywhere in the world we know. Instead of moving from the specific story to statements about the times, we might better move from the general observations of the story to the specific problems of our day. In this way we can see what illumination the one throws on the other, and we can test the relative truth of the story.

Another problem for the evaluator of literature—especially for the person who also trusts God's ultimate guidance of this earth—is that some of the literature we read seems to be entirely negative in its philosophy and emphasis. Why should a believer bother to read something like that? Shouldn't we read to be uplifted and encouraged? And when we do read a story that seems to work in direct conflict with our own beliefs, what are we to make of it? I want to offer three observations about this difficult issue.[12]

For one thing, some people seem to be totally convinced that contemporary fiction is only negative or full of violence and sex; so they don't want to read any of it and, as a consequence, miss out on some funny and quite affirmative stories. Faulkner gained notoriety early in his career as a writer of despair and decadence; the readers who ignored him missed a lot of hilariously funny tales from a master storyteller, and they also missed his consistent attempt to defend basic human values such as courage and honor and endurance.[13] Flannery O'Connor is often said to have written only of weird characters and desperate life situations. She did write stories that depicted human pain, but she was able, even in her grim tales, to capture with great humor the dialect and hypocrisy of some completely believable people. She claimed to write as she did in order to present the mystery of God's grace to modern readers.[14] The point is that there are funny and valuable stories in contemporary fiction; it is not by any means all grim and gruesome.[15]

For another thing, whether believers like to admit it or not, many people in this world live with despair and defeat, and they have no way of trusting God as a preserver of life—that is, they do not at all experience any preservation in their own stories. If a writer is attempting to picture life as it is for many people, he or she will have to show the suffering those people undergo. Some writers only see the grim side of things, to be sure, and some are bitter and defeated people themselves who find it only fitting to mock people who have a more optimistic outlook on life. One of literature's benefits is that it helps us to understand this world, even those parts of the world we wish we didn't have to see. Perhaps the one point of contact between this negative literature and our own experience of belief is that when we read of the defeated and hopeless people of the earth, we may come closer to grasping the meaning of the cross, the extent of God's willingness to know human experience at its extremity of forsakenness. Jesus had a hard time convincing people that he came not to the righteous but to the lost: the cross is the sign of God's movement to human despair and death. God knows the suffering of the world. In the most painful moments of our own lives, at our times of emptiness and dread, as well as in the negative and despairing literature we read, we see by faith that God is present, there on the cross, there in our suffering.

Third, because we are taking literature on its own terms as an independent field, and because, insofar as we are believers, we know that both our lives and this whole world are in God's loving hands, we

do not really need to have before us only positive, affirmative literature. It would be unrealistic to expect boundless affirmation in the
created order, which operates, after all, under limitations and ambiguity. We get our certainty and affirmation from God's Word within our
experience as believers. Some literature is affirmative about life, and
we can enjoy that when we find it. Our final critical question, however, is not (as some "Christian readers" would insist) is this story
positive or negative? Our final questions are more like these: Is this
story true to human experience? Is it told well enough to be convincing? Does it help us understand ourselves and our world a little better?
Some readers may decide they prefer not to read despairing literature,
having perhaps enough despair, or fear of it, in their own lives. That
decision is to be respected. Such a judgment, though, is not a necessary
consequence of believer's contact with negative opinions in literature.
Although it is perfectly acceptable for a given reader to reject a certain
type of literature, a critical stance that makes such a rejection stops
short of its job. Criticism is discriminating but inclusive. We do not
have to agree with a story's philosophy to recognize that it is a good
story.

Evaluation is not the last step of the critic. We read and discuss and
read again; all along the way we are making some judgments about
our reading, and if we read with other people, we will be testing those
judgments throughout our discussion. We do not evaluate so that we
can make definitive pronouncements about what we have read; rather,
we evaluate so that we can compare our judgments with those of other
readers and so that the benefits of literature are clearer to us. Evaluation is only a part of analysis and interpretation. We do it, as we do the
other interpretive functions, by using our imaginations, by thinking
and feeling, and by trying to understand our own reactions.

One critic has suggested that "we shall never know all about art or
the values of art until all art is at an end; meanwhile the artists will
continue to instruct us."[16] Such a notion clarifies again for us the
boundary within which all readers of literature must operate: we are
creatures of our own time and place, knowing neither all that has been
written or all that will be, living in a world teeming with energy and
imagination. The final word on our literature is yet to be spoken. New
stories will continually add to our knowledge, our experience, and our
standards of evaluation. Every critic works within those boundaries
that are themselves a part of our lives under God's preserving and
creating guidance. The reader who trusts God's guidance will not be
able to make surer evaluations than anyone else, but that reader may

well have a sense of those boundaries within which evaluation and analysis are carried out. That reader may also have other reasons for withholding final judgment until a future time when all the stories have been written. A good critic, believer or nonbeliever, will perceive that we cannot "know all about art . . . until all art is at an end." The reader who also trusts God's loving care of the world recognizes as well these two things: the whole story of humanity will not be known until all history is at an end; and we have had a preview of the ending in the story of Jesus. We have a gift of freedom in that trust. Not everything rides on our evaluations; no one standard of judgment can be absolute; we can read and make mistakes and change our minds and still enjoy the whole business.

If our evaluations are never really completed, we may feel uneasy about our role as readers and interpreters; if we analyze in the territory of freedom, we may begin to suspect our assignment is too open-ended. How do we manage to live with the risks of freedom? This is a question, of course, that goes far beyond the subject we are now facing. To approach this question, we need to think about how our lives in community help us with interpreting and trusting.

5

READING IN COMMUNITY

A reader guards against entirely subjective opinions about fiction by consulting other readers. For teachers or students, such exchange may take place in the classroom or during a coffee break or bull session. The academically inclined person might consult those readers who have published their judgments in scholarly journals; for others, a book club or a reading group will be the forum where people can talk about stories and try out the critic's tools. In some cities, the Sunday edition of the newspaper might still carry one or two reviews of current fiction, and educational radio might review books from time to time. It may be fair to say, however, that most readers will not have easy access to any so-called professional judgment about the fiction they want to read.

The purpose of this chapter is to discuss two issues centered on the idea of reading in community. A number of scholars recently have used the term "community of interpretation" for some specific purposes that will be noted below; I would like to apply the term now to the topic we have been examining. Approaching the idea, first, from the community's perspective rather than the reader's, we shall consider what it might mean for a reader to study literature through a community of interpretation and whether the church might serve as that community.

A COMMUNITY OF INTERPRETATION

Scholars from several different disciplines have used the phrase "community of interpretation." Professor Stanley Fish, for example, is a literary critic who has made an important case for the role of the reader in the task of literary criticism; he has also advanced the notion of a community of interpretation through which the reader understands both literature and the critical judgments about literature.[1] Fish is talking about what he calls an "informed reader" who is well trained and professionally competent in the use of the language, the elements of literature, and the business of criticism. Against critics who insist on the centrality of the objective text, Fish argues that the reader is necessarily and significantly involved in interpretation. The reader does not risk totally subjective judgments, however, since he or she will be a part of an interpretive community that will have been engaged over a long period of time in setting standards and refining literary principles. The informed reader, then, never acts alone but always interprets in the context of some tradition of understanding. In some ways, Fish's position seems addressed more decisively to an academic audience than to general readers. Most general readers may not have available to them so clearly defined and well-informed an interpretive community. My question is, Can the general reader, in any sense, find or form a valid and solidly useful community of interpretation?

Scholars from other disciplines have also discussed the role of a community in the work of interpretation. Theologian David Tracy talks about a "community of capable readers" that will verify an individual reader's decisions and help define which texts are to be called classics. For Tracy, interpretation is not complete until there has been dialogue with a larger community.[2] Ethicist Stanley Hauerwas reminds us that stories have within them the power of "producing a community of interpretation sufficient for the growth of further narratives," and he relates this to the ethical responsibilities of the church as a community of believers charged to tell the story of Jesus in such a way that the story will effect social justice.[3] What applications might those reflections have for our discussion of the relationship between theology and literature, for our consideration of story, church, and imagination?

As a person who trusts that God is both caring for the whole earth through those divine creative and preserving powers and caring for all believers through a loving and forgiving presence, the Christian lives in a specific community with others who also believe and trust God.[4] In that community the Christian regularly hears the ancient stories telling who God is and what God accomplishes and how much God promises and fulfills. The Christian hears those stories repeated in the lessons read during worship, in the sermon, in church school classes, in hymns and liturgies, in family devotions, and in private reading of the Bible. We are dependent on that rehearsal, for without it we would not only forget who God is but who we are as well. Those stories remind us that God is active in the lives of believers and is busy sustaining the creation; without those stories we would live in despair. Without the community of other believers, we would not know how to read those stories, and we would mistrust our own conclusions about God's love.

The community of believers provides the place where each individual believer is supported and encouraged. The support and encouragement grow out of the narratives with which the church is entrusted, and they take on power because of the imagination by which the church comprehends those narratives. The support is not simply, in other words, a matter of common human feeling, of holding one another's hands or having good times at parties, or feeding one another in moments of crisis—though all those things happen and are ingredients of the support. The heart of the matter is God's loving story. That record of God's consistent acceptance of rebellious people has been repeated and believed down through the centuries: it has been believed not as some idle hope, some dreamy wishfulness, but as a pattern borne out over and over in the experience of believers. I live from day to day not so much on my own confidence in God's love as on the confidence of Abraham and Ruth and Mary and Paul and Augustine and Theresa and Luther and Calvin and my grandmothers and my parents. These people believed God's promise and saw it enacted in their own lives and in the community of their day. It is the community's repetition of the story that keeps it fresh and vital for my life.

The community of believers also awakens the imagination of the individual believer and turns everyone into interpreters. When it fails to do these things, the community is both dull and faithless. It must awaken imagination because it is constantly bringing vividly into the present the record of God's faithful love, and because it knows that God the creator fills the earth with images and gives humans the gift of seeing them and shaping them and understanding them. New Testament scholar Amos Wilder has said that the "New Testament writings are in large part works of the imagination" because they present pictures and so enable us to see and believe.[5] The church tells the story with imagination; the believer uses the imagination to comprehend that story and to appropriate it for personal experience and to tell it again to others. The community turns everyone into interpreters. It has to be trying constantly to understand its own story; and, if it is genuinely a community, it will not rely on experts or authorities to do the interpreting but will develop the skills among the believers to read and analyze and understand and repeat. If only the pastor of a congregation can tell the story, then the congregation is only an audience and it will really grasp neither its foundations nor its mission; if only the pastor can tell the story, there may be no community. Therefore, the believers will not only hear but will also read and interpret; they will have the story deep within them so that they can remember it and retell it and enact it in the broader community of God's world.

Such a view of the church may seem idealistic and even unfamiliar. The church, too, after all, is made up of limited human beings who are at the same time believers and nonbelievers; the church is a community of saints and sinners. As an institution the church is both faithful to God's message of love and caught up in its own survival, property, and public image. Insofar as the church trusts God's love, it is the special people of God actively telling God's story to the world; insofar as the church trusts only itself and makes up its own stories, it is a rebellious and stubborn people destructive of the gospel. The church is always both. The church, too, lives in that strange place of tension, uncertain of its role in the world and brimming with confidence in God's mission—both at once. We know that the church is not always sparking our imaginations and inviting us to interpretation; we know that the congregation to which we belong may seem distant from our image of God's church, and we may wonder if our activity is even worth the effort. The weaknesses of human existence make such situations inevitable. The breadth of God's love, though, encourages us, compels us to hold on to that community, to keep telling God's story, and so be a part of the church becoming what it is called to be.

If the church is a community of believers that knows the gift of imagination and is accustomed to using it to interpret its own literature, then it can be a community of interpretation for Christians who also read other literature. Indeed, a part of the church's business—a neglected part, to be sure—is to be such a center for interpretation. This dimension of the church's mission may seem hard to justify: people know the church is supposed to tell the gospel story, and they can usually be convinced that the church should "help people"—at least to some degree. That the church should encourage and assist people in reading and interpreting contemporary fiction may seem as harebrained and inappropriate as the church having some role in political issues.

The case for the church's role as a community of interpretation for contemporary literature has to do with the fact that the God who rules over everyone and everything takes care of all the world as creator and preserver and of believers as divine lover and present forgiver. Everything in the order of creation, then, comes from God and is God's gift to the creatures. Literature is one of those gifts. The church is also one of God's gifts, designed especially by God as the place where the good news of love will be repeated and believers nurtured and commissioned. The church, however, cannot be indifferent to what goes on under God's other plan of caregiving; on the contrary, the church, because its members live under both plans, remains in dialogue with everything in the created order.

The church is not isolated from the world. Believers cannot live in isolation because they know who ultimately is directing everything, and they participate, right along with nonbelievers, in learning about and shaping the world. They may not be able to comprehend it and shape it as well as some of the nonbelievers. Taken together, if they were operating only on the basis of their beliefs, they might well bungle the whole thing. Luther advised against turning government over to Christians: since the world has in it both sheep and wolves, the sheep "would doubtless keep the peace and allow themselves to be fed and governed peacefully, but they would not live long."[6] Believers, however, will have their individual interests and talents and will be able to manage certain tasks with expertise. The church will count on believers who are informed citizens to help guide the state toward decisions of justice, and it will encourage them in that social responsibility. The church will also count on believers who are informed readers to be responsible literary critics. It's all a matter of the care of the earth.

We are not obligated, however, to leave everything to the experts—not interpretation of the gospel, not political decisions, not the reading of literature. The believer is a citizen who understands that the earth is God's: he or she may not know all the intricacies of nuclear energy or the complexities of the economy. Still, the care of the earth suggests, in the most unmistakable way, the avoidance of nuclear catastrophe and the maintenance of a just, equitable economic order. The believer may not know precisely how to reach these goals, but he or she can be sure that they are legitimate goals and can study the issues, talk with other believers and with experts, and make thoughtful recommendations for establishment of policy. Such judgments are completely within the believer's territory, since he or she knows that the earth is God's.

In much the same way, the believer who is a reader of literature knows that the earth is God's and the imagination one of God's gifts. That believer may not have read all the literary theories from Aristotle to Northrop Frye and Stanley Fish but will nonetheless recognize that in literature a person deals with the gifts of God, the power of narrative, and the wonder of imagination. The believer will be aware of the benefits of literature, the ways it can entertain us, help us understand our world and ourselves, and hold before us enduring values. Any reader can come to see those advantages of literature, and the reader who is a believer, while not necessarily able to interpret more accurately than anyone else, certainly has every reason to derive as much from contemporary literature as possible. Insofar as he or she is just a reader, unconcerned with matters of belief, that reader will be able to read all alone or perhaps with some standard critical tools and will depend on whatever interpretations may be available through general resources; insofar as that reader is also a believer, the existence of a community of believers will be a major support for interpretation.

A COMMUNITY INTERPRETING
THE BIBLE

We are moving toward seeing how the believers who are also readers of contemporary fiction might form a small community of interpretation, from which they will do their reading and together learn more about themselves and God's world. First, however, we want to gain a broader view of the whole congregation as an interpretive community. In what sense does the congregation have that potential, and what difference will such a role make for an understanding of the relationship between literature and theology?

When the church acts as an interpretive community, precisely there the individual believer begins to develop the abilities and the courage to become an interpreter, not only within the context of the believing family but also, more broadly, in God's created territory. The church, then, prepares us for service in the world.

The Church Studying the Bible

Much of what I said earlier about interpretation—both its difficulties and its possibilities—can be applied to the church's interpretation of the Bible. We can listen on Sunday morning to the texts as they are read, study some passages in a church school, and read occasionally at home; but when we come to puzzles, we may simply assume that they are beyond us and are to be left to scholars and critics for solution and illumination. We may turn to a Bible dictionary or commentary if we have one at home, but we sense that even then we are only getting one opinion and that there must surely be many more which, even if we knew about them, we might not comprehend. For many folks in the church today, the Bible is an unreadable book of puzzles that we approach with a sense of inadequacy, strongly convinced of our limitations, willing to get what we can but doubting that we will be able to understand what we read, and perhaps feeling a little useless about the whole enterprise.

One way to overcome this sense of inadequacy and to strengthen the church's function as a community of interpretation is to apply basic interpretive skills to the Bible itself.[7] This is not simply a Bible-as-literature approach: that approach can lead to misunderstanding if it means putting the Bible into a second-class position or if it implies that the Bible is not therefore authoritative. The Bible does have some features in common with other literature, however: principally its use of distinct literary elements such as narrative, imagery, allusion, characterizations, and so on. The Bible does have authority: the Bible is God's story, it is God's special vehicle for the proclaiming of good news. At the same time, it is literature, and we can use some of the same proficiency in interpreting the Bible that we use in interpreting other literature. Curiously enough, biblical stories, for the most part, are told with a straightforward and unusually clear style. Even when the stories involve complexities of plot or characterization, we can tell what is happening and have a basic grasp of the story's meaning and purpose without a great deal of technical background. Thus, children are able to hear and remember the great narratives. The complexities may not come through to us until we are older and more experienced with both reading and living, but the narrative sticks and so supports us in faith. (The contemporary writer Reynolds Price has done a translation of some biblical narratives and published them under the title *A Palpable God*. As a writer of narratives himself and as a person who grew up in the storytelling culture of the Southern United States, Price found himself drawn to these sacred narratives because of their clarity and their essential truthfulness.)

Narrative itself holds deep significance for us all. Once upon a time, we seemed to think stories were for children and that adults should thrive on abstractions. Increasingly, we are realizing that all people need and love stories. We human beings apparently think in stories, learn by stories, understand ourselves and our world by stories, and are incurable listeners to and tellers of stories.[8] The importance of narrative in the Bible, then, only underscores and reinforces what is an observable human characteristic. Reynolds Price has noted that, whether one is an effective storyteller or a careful listener, a strong narrative can help human beings survive; he points out that this feature of the story was as important in biblical times as it is today.[9] We can talk about the value of narrative for us in many different ways: it can help us make it through our lives with some sense of purpose and a measure of happiness; it can establish order in our confused existence; it can help us relate abstract ideas to our ordinary experience, to explain and represent values so that other people might know more clearly what we want to communicate; it can give ways to remember and to imagine.

The main thesis here is that believers can indeed interpret their own special literature. For one thing, they, like all other people, are story lovers; for another, they are a people born of a magnificent story. We have both tools and reasons for being interpreters. We can read the Bible and comprehend a great deal of it without having been to seminary and without constantly burrowing through volumes of commentaries and dictionaries. Not only can we read and comprehend, it is really part of our purpose as a community of believers to be able to interpret this literature. If we remain biblically illiterate, as many today say we are, then we are no better off than the church of the Middle Ages: we are victims of what some expert or huckster might try to sell, and we cannot possibly pass along to the next generation a story which has supported and sustained us.

Why is it that the book which gives us life is so unfamiliar to us today? One problem is that we are handicapped even by the way the Bible is used in the church. In worship, the offenses are most serious. The Bible is often read without feeling and without precision: the reader (pastors included) often seems not to have bothered to read through the text before stepping to the lectern and, more often, has not looked up the pronunciation of difficult words or thought about inflection. We hear snippets and are not given any hint about the context from which those pieces come. Often the pastor doesn't preach on the text; if the pastor claims to be preaching on the text, we may not recognize how the text relates to what is being preached. The lectionary, although it does now have some readings continued from Sunday to Sunday from a single book, still is necessarily chopped into units that may not always fit together. In church school classes, we sometimes approach Scripture in the same way, through brief passages isolated from their context; sometimes these classes are taught by people who, though dedicated and able, are concerned with defending a literal interpretation of the text. The result of all this is that the Bible becomes, even for the church, a dead book.

If, however, we can use our imaginations in reading, preaching, and teaching, then perhaps those biblical narratives and the whole great drama of God's loving activity for us can begin to come alive again. We do this by studying the text, by examining its literary components, by trying to see what the story is and what it might have meant to the original hearers or readers, as well as what it might mean for us. We do this by inviting the hearers to use their own imaginations. We do it by evoking details, by presenting personalities, by letting the characters of the biblical story exist in the depth of their own human problems. For the Bible to be for us the lively narrative it really is, it has to be more than a book of records or a source of dogma; it must be the narrative of faith, received, believed, trusted by countless communities of believers down through the ages. So, our imaginations are activated to see the story of faith worked out in succeeding generations right up to our own. God's gift of imagination helps us to make the connections, to move from the reality presented in those chronicles of faith to the realities in which we live day by day.

How are we to overcome the difficulties of understanding a complicated book? How are we to be a community of interpretation of the very literature with which we are entrusted? One way might be for a group of believers to focus their attention on some biblical narratives. As a group, you might select several specific stories for your study. At the beginning you would analyze relatively short stories, such as an episode in the life of some biblical personality, or one of Jesus' parables. Later you could tackle an entire narrative, such as the Book of Ruth, the Joseph or David stories, or the Gospel of Mark. Once you agree on a narrative for your study, read the story looking for answers to basic literary questions (such as those we discussed in chapters 3 and 4). You might outline some of those questions for the class in a form like this:

1. What are the essential elements of the plot?
2. What is the setting of the story, and how important is it to the action and characters?
3. Who are the characters? How would you describe the main character(s)? Do any surprising personality features appear? Are the characters stereotypes or complex persons? Are there minor characters who have special roles?
4. Where do you see conflict in the story? In the ideas? Between two characters or groups? Within a character?
5. Do you see any instance of the use of irony?

6. Are there particular images, symbols, or allusions which are significant for the story?
7. Do you observe any parallels or contrasts within the narrative?
8. Can you tell what attitude the author has toward this account or toward these characters?
9. Can you imagine how the story might be different if you were to retell it from the perspective of one of the characters?
10. What is the theme, main idea, or purpose of the narrative?

You can accomplish a great deal in this way without the use of interpretive aids, but you may want to check the resources in your church or public library for additional information. Perhaps you would do this after you have been through the narrative once and dealt with the major literary issues. You might give some brief assignments to class members. One person might read about the story in a general commentary (such as *The Interpreter's Bible*); someone else might look up difficult terms or names in a Bible dictionary; others could follow up biblical parallels or references (cited in the margins of many editions of the Bible); still others could find locations on a map or in a Bible atlas. You might be sure that several translations of the Bible are being used in the class so that you can get different perspectives on how the text might be read. You might also consult some modern retelling of the biblical stories, such as Price's *A Palpable God*, Elie Wiesel's *Messengers of God*, or Clarence Jordan's "Cotton-Patch New Testament."[10]

As you talk about the story, you need not feel you have to deal with all the literary questions or solve every riddle. Select, rather, those issues that seem most interesting to you or most important to the story. Once you have discussed the narrative (or perhaps somewhere during the discussion), ask yourself three additional questions:

11. In what ways does this particular story reflect, interpret, or expand God's great story of creating, preserving, delivering, forgiving, and freeing?
12. Do you see any parallels between the short narrative before you and the story of the cross and resurrection of Jesus Christ?
13. In what ways does the biblical narrative reflect or help you understand your own personal story or your community's story?

Such a procedure might be a little different from what many church school classes are accustomed to, but it could have some advantages. A group might be able to operate with a moderator and thus not need a highly qualified and hard-to-get "teacher." Over a period of time, the group might develop a strong feeling for God's great story. They might be strengthened in their confidence about what is at the heart of the church's mission. The process might encourage individual participation in the learning experience; it might help people read the Bible on their own; it might make them familiar with resources in their church library. Such study of the Bible, using abilities that many people already have, might help church members see themselves as a community of interpretation, as a group of people who know the book that is the source of strength for their lives and a people who can read and appreciate it and make applications to their own place and time. Following hard upon knowledge of God's story would be a conviction about the mission of the church, attention to the needs of all God's people, and imaginative, compelling ministry.

The Preacher Telling Stories

The preacher is the chief storyteller of the community of believers. Others in the community will tell the story, but the preacher is charged with the story, commissioned to tell it publicly, worship service after worship service, so that the community is encouraged and sustained by it. Such things as the reading of lessons in the worship service and the preaching of the sermon become, therefore, means by which the imagination of the community may be enriched, interpretive skills demonstrated, and the community of storytellers nurtured.

Novelist John Gardner has made the point that the poet's task is to celebrate the work of a hero or heroine.[11] The church, the community of believers, has always done this by retelling stories of God's mighty acts in which God is the heroic figure who causes and suffers and celebrates the changes in the world. Sometimes those stories also celebrate the work of women and men who live in the confidence of God's love and of God's firm control of this world. In whatever ways the shorter narratives may make their contributions, the great dramatic story is really the powerful tale of God's activity moving through human history, sometimes on tiptoe, sometimes with swash-buckling boldness. This is the story—whatever else we may have to say—that undergirds our preaching. Where it is missing, the sermon may well be flat and empty.

Today's sermons occasionally leave aside the great biblical narrative and with it the individual scriptural texts. Sometimes a preacher settles for moral teachings that are, compared to those memorable biblical stories, totally forgettable. Some preachers seem to prefer what is often called a "topical sermon," that is, one which abstracts a topic from a biblical text and focuses wholly on that topic. Because of the abstraction, the topical sermon is usually itself forgettable. In an effort to make it memorable, the preacher punctuates it with little stories even further removed from the biblical narrative. The stories themselves may be memorable (some congregations can remember hearing them over and over from several different preachers and once in a while, across the years, from the same preacher), but they are usually memorable only for themselves and seldom for the point the preacher is trying to make. A sermon, punctuated by anecdotes, may look something like this:

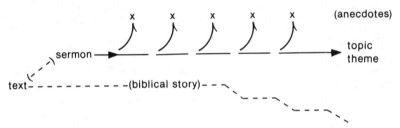

One of the problems with this pattern is that there is a direct correlation between the appearance of the anecdotes and the congregation's attention level: that is, when the little stories appear, the attention is high, and when the stories end, the attention drops off. It is as though the mind were saying, OK, the entertainment is over; we're heading back to abstractions, and I can shift into neutral. If the story is compelling enough, of course, the mind may stay with it or wander onto paths to which the story leads. Meanwhile, the preacher goes on trying to make the abstract point that the story was intended to illustrate. The result is that if indeed the illustrations are there to demonstrate a point—a point somehow expressed in between the illustrations—the congregation is not attentive at precisely the time the preacher wants it to be attentive. When I speak of the preacher telling stories, this is *not* what I mean. Such a use of stories does indicate the power of narrative, but in this case the preacher is often using the story as an entertaining device to hold the audience's attention until something more substantive can be presented. That abuses both the audience and the nature of narrative itself.

In contrast to this, we might aim for a sermon that develops, grows, has suspense, holds the listener, has its own unity. This suggests a form very much like a story, a form that in itself builds toward a climax and keeps the audience interested in seeing how the unfolding narrative will be resolved. How does the preacher accomplish this? Basic to the task is a thorough examination of the text. The preacher might well use some of the same techniques that would be used in a reader's analysis of literature or the community of believers' interpretation of a biblical story. In any case, the preacher will be attentive to narrative form and to the power of the story.

Many books have been written now about narrative preaching; they are, of course, varied in their emphases.[12] Important for our purposes here are three points, and all three are related to our discussion of the relationship between literature and theology.

1. As the preacher understands more and more the way stories work and how they might be interpreted, he or she will be able to present a narrative effectively in the pulpit. The text, especially when it is in narrative form, might well supply the framework for the sermon. This does not mean simply retelling the biblical narrative; if the preacher does that without some new approach, some new purpose, some new perspective, he or she will most certainly lose the attention of those who have heard the story a hundred times before. So the preacher may let the plot of the biblical story serve as an outline for the sermon, but that plot will always be expanded, exploded, so that the new hearers might catch something of its original power.

2. A work of contemporary literature might furnish an interesting counterpoint to a biblical narrative or might be perceived as a modern interpretation of a biblical theme. In such a case, the preacher might tell the modern story—giving full credit to the writer, of course, and recognizing that in this retelling the story becomes, in some ways, different from the story its author told. The preacher might tell the modern story and at its conclusion draw together explicitly the connections with the biblical narrative. Or the preacher might risk simply telling the modern story and letting the congregation make its own connections.

3. Yet another possibility might be for the preacher to think of the sermon as a kind of narrative.[13] Even where there is no "once upon a time," no characterization, no story, the sermon might still have within it some elements of narrative: it might lay grounds of suspense at the outset by raising questions that the congregation would like to see answered; it might let the congregation in on the issues that enter the preacher's mind about a text as the preacher prepares for the sermon; it might employ images and make allusions and encourage the listeners to use their imaginations.

When the preacher manages in some way to be a storyteller, more is happening than the mere entertainment of a congregation. If the preacher can begin to build, over a period of time, a sensitivity toward the larger story of God's love, then the congregation itself comes to know that story more intimately and is able to tell it more faithfully, both for its own nourishment and for its testimony to others. If the preacher is attentive to the stories of the modern world, stories that may have their origins in God's preserving way of managing this earth, then the congregation may extend its attention to its own life and experience as carried out in the world. If the preacher can demonstrate Sunday after Sunday a way of interpreting God's great story, then the congregation too may fulfill its task of being the community of interpretation and may learn more easily how to understand the texts that are its source and strength.

A COMMUNITY INTERPRETING MODERN STORIES

Because at the very center of its own existence the church listens to stories and tells them, the church becomes a likely place for the interpretation of modern stories. In the context of their own community of interpretation, believers who are also readers of contemporary fiction might come together to read and imagine and think. In the process, they may understand one another, themselves, and their world a little better, and they may find their values reinforced or held up for question; as a hidden bonus, they might awake prepared for hearing and telling anew God's refreshing words of love.

For the reader to approach literature through a community of interpretation would offer a number of advantages. It would mean, for example, that the reader would have another set of imaginations through which to filter this experience: more points of contact with varied realities, more memories. It would mean more resources and richer reading background for understanding allusions and symbols. It would mean checks and balances against wild-eyed readings, and it would mean a safe place to test ideas and risk personal judgments. A community of interpretation would be a place where a reader could find support and acceptance and mutual interests and a common background for understanding. It would provide a way of parceling out assignments for covering the investigation of a text.

Such a group might well exist within a congregation or among believers from several congregations. It might take the form of a class, either for academic credit or as extracurricular activity, in a college or seminary. Each set of readers would have to decide its own ground rules, of course, and might want to check out commonly held assumptions at the beginning of the study. If these readers were all members of the same congregation, they might meet at some time set aside within the church school, but they may also want to meet outside the traditional structure. Whatever arrangements were made, the congregation might well recognize this study to be an appropriate part of the congregation's extension into God's world, learning from it and participating in shaping it.

General Guidelines

A study of this sort might well deal with serious literature and serious issues, but the group should try not to take itself too seriously and should aim at having some fun. The following guidelines are not a set of procedures which would stifle the very creativity a community of interpretation could foster: they are only suggestions as to how that community might go about its task.

1. Review skills of literary interpretation.
2. Discuss the purposes of literature.
3. Discuss what you expect to get out of the study.
4. Agree on a reading list: you might consider reading a number of works by a single author or varying the types of stories you read (comedy, tragedy, satire).
5. Assign tasks so as to spread outside work around: someone might read brief biographical accounts, someone else might make an initial search on allusions.
6. Vary the emphasis or approach from one session to the next: one time you might concentrate on understanding the main characters in the story; another time you could work toward a statement of the story's theme.
7. Examine the various fictional elements you find in the story.
8. Practice unraveling small sections (the opening paragraph, material at the climax).
9. Remember to examine the work as a whole, not just its isolated parts.
10. See if you can determine the particular benefits of the story you are reading.
11. Resist forming a single "Christian" meaning, but pursue parallels and links to belief which readers have noticed.
12. Allow plenty of room for differences of opinion, and don't try to force uniform conclusions.

13. As the group is willing, let the work carry you into personal stories and deeper levels of meaning.
14. Discuss where the work leads you.
15. Enjoy.

Analyzing Biblical and
Theological Allusions

Most of these points should be fairly evident strategies, based on the discussion we have had in this volume so far. With those general guidelines in mind, we can now be more specific about some of the exercises readers might perform. We discussed earlier the importance of allusion as one of the major elements of fiction, and we have noted the possibilities of allusions prodding our imaginations. Now we can go into more detail. When you come across an allusion to some biblical or theological material, what exactly do you do with it? How can you be faithful to the integrity of the literature and still do justice to the background of the allusion? Again, I would insist that the way you handle it has nothing to do with whether or not you hold the Bible to be authoritative or the theology credible; it has much more to do with responsible techniques of literary criticism. Your belief and background in the literature of faith may mean, however, that you have a head start in figuring out the allusion's purpose because you already know the sources; or they may mean that you will feel more deeply attracted to those allusions because they approach what is already significant in your life. At any rate, what should we be watching for? How do we perform this particular operation in a territory where the two fields of literature and theology seem to come together most forcefully? Here are some of the steps you might take, though they will not apply equally to all works of literature—and, of course, they are not to be followed only in this order or in any slavish fashion.

1. Identify the allusion and mark its context carefully. How do you know it is a biblical or theological allusion? Is it a direct quote from the Bible, from hymnody or liturgy? Is it a specific reference to some traditional Christian doctrine? You might distinguish between explicit and implicit allusions, justifying the implicit ones by as much of the context as possible.
2. Trace the allusion in the story itself. Does it appear more than once? If so, note its context in each instance and determine whether or not the usage is consistent. Is it associated with a particular character? If so, how does the allusion relate to that character's development?

3. Trace the allusion outside the story. If necessary, use a biblical concordance or a theological dictionary. This may well involve more than casual reading of a verse or two. Suppose a character in the story has a biblical name, for example; then you need to know about the biblical character by that name and that character's story. If you are dealing with some point of doctrine, you will need to think not only about how that doctrine has been stated traditionally but also how it might have developed through the years, what its original purpose was, and how it might have been understood in the specific historical period of the story you are reading. If in a Flannery O'Connor story, for example, you come across a Jesuit talking about penitence, it will help if you know something about Jesuits as well as about the Roman Catholic church's concept of penitence.

4. Try to relate the information you have discovered to the story itself, and see how the allusion is being used. If the character in your story has a biblical name, in what ways is the author using that name to contribute to the development of his or her character? You may find that the name is incidental and so is not really an allusion after all. Or you may find there is some irony suggested in the usage. What does it mean when Faulkner names the progenitor of the infamous Snopes clan Abraham? Does it mean any more than that he is the head of a great tribe? Is there contrast implied between Abraham's history as a hero of faith and Ab Snopes's record of deceit and shiftlessness, or is there something about Ab's fierce determination that is not unlike Abraham's? Would it help to know that, in an early draft, Faulkner entitled one of his first stories about Ab "Father Abraham"?[14] You see from this brief example that there will be many conceivable angles and so great necessity for close reading and adroit interpretation. You are trying to determine, as best you can, with what evidence you have from the text, whether the allusion adds some value to the narrative by reaching outside the immediate setting and presenting an enriching contrast, or whether perhaps the allusion is ironical, suggesting that the source itself does not have the value in the minds of the characters or the author that it might have for you.

5. Step back from the allusion and try to see how its appearance in the story relates to the whole narrative before you. Is there any pattern within the story into which this allusion might fit directly? Is this the only allusion with biblical or theological con-

tent in the story, and if so, is it simply an isolated and relatively incidental reference? Or is there a pattern of allusions, and do they fit together? *Do they help you understand what the story is about?* Without this final step, we have not dealt fairly with the literature, since it does not exist for its parts, after all, but for the whole. One criticism of so-called religious interpretation of literature is that it frequently seems to focus on a piece of the story and then leap to its own conclusions rather than let an examination of the pieces move toward comprehension of the whole. Such a mistaken approach might look something like this:

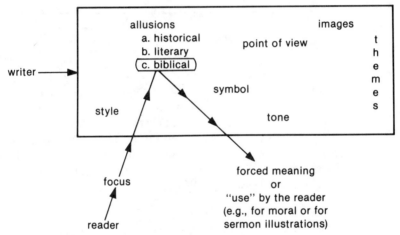

Complete Short Story

A literary critic who appreciates the integrity of the work of literature and has a sense of the wholeness of the narrative, on the other hand, will take all the parts into consideration and try to see in what ways they may add up to a thematic statement, or in what ways the parts work together, or how the whole story might be enjoyed. In the first illustration, the reader focuses on only one element of the story and forces a meaning from that element, in disregard of the other elements and for the major purpose of finding a desired "use" that will fit the reader's present interests. In the second illustration, below, the reader keeps a focus on the whole story, tries to see relationship between the parts, allows the various elements to function as they will, and lets the story unfold consistently with its own development. In the second illustration, then, the picture of the story is the same; what is different is the reader's point of focus.

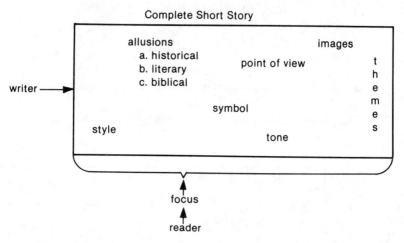

There is no guarantee, of course, that the reader will make the right decisions about the allusions in a story, but the reader is likely to come close if he or she will check the context, trace the allusion as it is used in the story and in its background outside the story, and give the allusion its place in the entire narrative. Interpretation always involves an interplay between the whole narrative and its various parts.[15]

Analyzing Opening Paragraphs

Another exercise that might prove helpful to a group of readers would be to analyze carefully a particular section of a story (guideline 8 above). Readers may find it especially interesting to take a close look at the opening paragraphs of a narrative, since often a writer will set the stage for later developments in those first lines. In order to make this analysis, you would be remembering all your interpretive techniques and applying them all in a short portion of the text. You would note which characters are introduced at the beginning and how they are presented. You would watch carefully for the initial tone of the work. You would look for symbols and images and allusions that might prepare you for what is to come in the narrative. You could see if a particular word or phrase is repeated in the opening sentences, since that repetition might give you a hint about the meaning of the story.

If you are reading in a group, you might copy the opening few paragraphs out on another page, typed with double-spacing so that each reader would have room to make notations. You might circle key images, underline characters' names, box allusions, and note in the margins your impressions about point of view, irony, or setting. By making such a concentrated attack on one brief section of a story, you could be more thorough in your discussion and prepare the way for analysis of the total narrative. You could compare the opening sections with the closing sections. Are key words repeated? Have you been prepared from the beginning for what happens at the end? Does the story come full circle in any sense?

Not every story will lend itself to this type of analysis of the opening passages. Someone in the group would have to read the story before you decided to approach your discussion of it in this way. In any story, however, you could submit the narrative to this same scrutiny: you could select some decisive passage, perhaps a scene at the climax, and go over it carefully, not only trying to see how the fictional elements work within it but also asking how it fits in its particular position in the narrative, how it serves to move the story toward resolution or to illuminate the development of a character. Usually we do not have time for such close reading; occasionally, though, it can be instructive and enjoyable to concentrate on a short passage, combing it for all it is worth.

Following the Story's Leads

When a group reads and discusses literature, it may not be satisfied simply to close the book and forget its experience. I should say something, then, about guideline 14: Where does the story lead you? Since literature is not an end in itself, you might want to determine whether there are steps beyond your reading and discussion. A given story might, for example, open your awareness to some social problem, and you might decide to learn more about that problem, what form it takes in your own community, and what you might be able to do about it. Another story might lead you to some discovery about yourself that would need exploration in more detail: perhaps the group could help; perhaps a counselor would be valuable. The story might lead you to other reading: another story by the same writer, another story on the same theme or type of people or section of the country or time in history. You might want to see if the story has ever been made into a film, and, if it has, you might view the film together for another kind of imaginative experience. Sometimes a story might lead you to review a biblical narrative or a point of

Christian belief. If you read an account of a person burdened by guilt or feeling determined by a hostile fate, you could explore the church's perception of those issues. When that sort of thing happens, the literature will have primed you for growth in faith; it may not have given answers, but it will have led you to deeper questioning. That is part of the purpose of the dialogue. It is not the only purpose, you will remember, because you will also be enjoying the material and learning about yourself and the world and human values, but occasionally a story may put you in the position to make a connection with your own trust in God's care for us all. At that point you can count especially on your community of interpretation to move with you into God's great narrative, and interpretation will lead to interpretation, imagination to imagination, faith to faith.

Getting Started

With an enormous world of creative literature available to you and with new books coming on the market every week, where are you to begin? How do you get started as a community of interpretation for modern literature?

You could start any one of a thousand places, of course. If you are reading with a group of people, you will want, quite naturally, the whole group to help set the direction. Someone in the group may be an inveterate reader and may have a year's supply of novels on the tip of the tongue. You may decide to study some of the classics of literature, renewing acquaintance with authors you haven't read since high school or exploring the great books of a culture unfamiliar to you. You could always start with the best seller list: you would find some good books there, and you would be more familiar with what many people today are reading; but you may also waste some time wading through long—and perhaps, ultimately trivial—tales which offer more entertainment than substance. Getting started will not be a major problem. Even if you feel you know absolutely nothing about which writers are worth reading today, you will find that you can quickly draw up a list of suggestions by pooling the experience in the group or by consulting local bookdealers, librarians, or reviewers. Part of the fun is discovery.

Part II

In this part, I will examine the works of some twentieth-century writers who have told their stories about life in the Southern part of the United States. The following chapters provide—and this is their primary purpose—a means of illustrating some of the skills and problems discussed in part I. To be sure, any collection of literature, any group of stories, could serve that purpose. Questions of interpretation remain the same whether one talks about the tragedies of Shakespeare, the Romantic poems of Keats or Shelley, the absurd theater of Samuel Beckett, the ancient comedies of Aristophanes, or the contemporary works of William Gass or Thomas Pynchon. Some literature may offer more substance than another, may have proven itself by enduring, may have a stronger critical reputation; but thousands upon thousands of poems, plays, novels, and short stories could be examined and readily repay the effort.

In the present study, I have chosen to concentrate on five Southern writers for a variety of reasons. For one thing, using writers from the same region, of the same time period, working in the same genre, allows me to sharpen the focus and establish some unity for the discussion; it narrows what could be an extremely broad field of inquiry. For another, Southern writing has within it the varied interests and universal appeal one should expect from any solid literary collection. For yet another, Southern fiction offers many points of connection with the basic concerns of this book. The concentration on Southern literature, however, does not arise from parochialism, nor does it necessarily imply that Southern literature is superior to the writing from other regions.

Other regions have also produced significant creative works, of course. In the early years of this country's history, New England was the literary capital, the fertile region for poetry, essays, and fiction; the

104

Midwest has provided numerous major American writers; and with all that has been written in this country over the past two hundred years, many states and sections can claim honor for their own literature. To talk about the importance of Southern literature in no way diminishes the value of those other regional expressions. Still, one can recognize the strength of the Southern literary tradition. This is a tradition that became clear in the 1920s and 1930s with the work of people like William Faulkner, Allen Tate, John Crowe Ransom, Ellen Glasgow, and Thomas Wolfe; but its roots go back to William Byrd and Thomas Jefferson, to Edgar Allan Poe, William Gilmore Simms, and Henry Timrod, to humorists such as Augustus Baldwin Longstreet, Johnson Jones Hooper, and George Washington Harris. That rich heritage has been continued through the fiction of Caroline Gordon, Flannery O'Connor, Walker Percy, Katherine Anne Porter, William Styron, Peter Taylor, Robert Penn Warren, Eudora Welty, and Richard Wright; it is being expanded by a new generation of writers like Doris Betts, Fred Chappell, James Dickey, Ernest J. Gaines, George Garrett, Gail Godwin, Guy Owen, Reynolds Price, Anne Tyler, Alice Walker, and many others.[1]

The question of what makes these people Southern writers—beyond the matter of their birth in Southern states—remains too complicated for this brief overview; that is the question of what Southern literature is really all about. Scholars who have analyzed this wealth of material have often listed the themes that most frequently appear: the role of slavery and the Civil War, the attachment to the land, the devotion to family and community, the deep Protestant background, the air of violence, the influence of history, the strain of individualism, the love of talking and storytelling, the self-consciousness about the region, and the identity within a somewhat uniform culture. These themes— so briefly stated, of course—may begin to sound like clichés. It should be obvious that any body of literature, developed over a period of so many years by so many individual talents, cannot be easily and neatly categorized. Furthermore, people who are writing currently will bring new perspectives to old issues—as we shall see in the following chapters. Few Southern writers are interested in all those themes; but as one reads this literature one is struck by how many times some of those issues surface in one form or another. I want to guard against generalizing and oversimplifying. At the same time, it is important to point out that some of the themes traditionally associated with Southern literature are particularly appropriate to the concerns of this book.

Southern literature, for example, has preserved a strong devotion to storytelling. As we shall see, a number of Southern writers recognize the value of their own families having been made up of storytellers and yarn-spinners. This attention to narrative continues to hold, despite what some scholars see as a nonnarrative direction in much modern fiction. Nathan Scott has observed that, while theologians are finding renewed interest in narrative, many modern writers are more and more skeptical of traditional narrative forms. Their skepticism is related to doubts about order and sensibleness in the universe. A clear narrative structure or a well-developed plot seems to suggest that something about life makes sense, has limits and meaning. Some people today, as was noted in chapter 1, have trouble experiencing order and meaning in this world; writers can express the disorder and meaninglessness they feel by writing fiction that does not conform to traditional narrative elements, that expresses an unstable, confusing, and purposeless universe.[2] Southern writers, for the most part, maintain their appreciation of narrative and traditional elements of fiction. This does not mean that all Southern writers find meaning and purpose in life: there are skeptics among them, too, even when they adhere to more conventional narrative techniques. Southern literature's general attraction to narrative does provide, however, a clear link with an interest Christians also have in storytelling.

Southern literature's devotion to narrative is related to its devotion to history. For many Southern writers, the past holds enormous significance: the victories and the defeats, the glory and the shame, the romanticism and the bitter irony. For some writers, it is by reviewing, analyzing, and maybe even wallowing in the past that Southerners come to understand who they are and what their lives mean. In Robert Penn Warren's novel *All the King's Men*, Jack Burden, caught up in Louisiana politics in the 1930s, can only tell his story by also trying to discover what happened to his own ancestors during the American Civil War; his own identity might be clarified by the identity of his forebears.[3] Quentin Compson, in Faulkner's *Absalom, Absalom!* seems compelled to explore and understand the story of Thomas Sutpen and his family, most of whom had died twenty years before Quentin was born.[4] Christians may not be attracted to history for quite the same reasons Southerners seem to be, but Christians do value their past, both the great story of God's activity as recorded in Scripture and the tales of other believers down through the centuries. Readers who are Christians may find, again, some common ground with a dimension of Southern literature.

Southern writers' high regard for community establishes still another connection with Christian interests. For many Southern writers, it isn't just that the South is important as a community of values and common assumptions; it is also that their town or their county is important. Characters in stories often express this identity with their neighbors: people of a community band together to support one another in the face of an enemy. Sometimes a story may even be told from the perspective of the community, as though the story took its shape not alone through the consciousness of a single storyteller; rather as the people of the town told and retold a tale, guessed about what had happened, passed on rumors, and made their own interpretations—as all that took place, a certain community consciousness developed, a common story evolved and could be spoken as though with one voice.[5] An absorption with a single vision of reality might mean dangerous chauvinism or destructive narrow-mindedness, and that happens in Southern towns and states just as it happens in other regions and in the church. There are negative as well as positive dimensions to this concern with community. The point here is that modern readers who are Christians will find some common interests with Southern writers who recognize both the benefits and the limitations of one's community.

The role of Christianity itself within the South constitutes another bond. Many observers talk about the dominance of Protestantism in the region, the influence of Calvin, the place of sin and guilt, or the area's Bible-belt identity. Flannery O'Connor once called the South "Christ-haunted."[6] Intriguing as that description is, it is not an easy assessment to evaluate. One would need to determine both what she meant by the term and to what extent she might be right. Yet it is clear that religion has been an influential force in the South. There are, however, striking differences between any culture's appropriation of Christianity, on the one hand, and the gospel story that lies at the center of the Christian faith on the other. There is another of literature's rewards: it invites the reader into that confrontation of gospel and culture. The reader who trusts God's care of all that is finds deepening complications: God watches over, preserves, uses the society and its literature, and God judges. At the same time, God loves and calls into distinctive, freeing mission those groups of believers who will live in the society, read, enjoy, and be confounded by its literature. So there is a tension field again. Because the South is aware of evil and human sinfulness (for good or ill, however sharp or dull the definitions, Southerners know about sin), perhaps the South supplies a good image of the tension in which all believers live.

In the following chapters, we will look at the fiction of five Southern writers. One of these is William Faulkner, the master storyteller who won international appreciation and whose fiction set a standard for Southern literature that intimidates or inspires those writers who come after him. The second, Flannery O'Connor, despite the relatively small volume of her fiction—two short novels and two collections of short stories—seems assured an honored place in American literature. Both Faulkner and O'Connor died in the 1960s. The final three writers— Ernest J. Gaines, Alice Walker, and Reynolds Price—may not be as familiar to most readers. They are still writing, and the critical verdict is not yet in. They are our contemporaries, however, and have their own ways of helping us know ourselves and our world.

In these remaining chapters, I intend to apply some of the principles we have discussed in part I. I will not attempt to be exhaustive in treating a particular story; I mean more to give examples of how a reader might approach a piece of fiction. Questions about biblical allusions and religious issues will be of concern, since those questions inevitably arise and have peculiar complexities. By giving them so much attention, however, I may seem to contradict my emphasis on their place as one segment of the larger interpretive exercise. I hope to show how they might be handled and, in the process, make clear that they are indeed only one part of the whole critical task. I will face some of those difficult points of interpretation; but the commentary is not so much authoritative conclusion as starting ground for your own reading and discussion. I will not summarize the story, except in the most cursory way. I encourage you to read the story and make your own judgments. What has gone before has only been preparation for the pleasure of the literature itself.

6

WILLIAM FAULKNER
"UNCLE WILLY"

In many of his stories, William Faulkner used specifically Christian references and images. His early novel *The Sound and the Fury* (1927) is divided into four major sections, each given a date on an Easter weekend; *Light in August* (1932) has as one of its central characters a man named Joe Christmas, whose life story, at a few points, may remind readers of New Testament accounts of Jesus; *A Fable* (1954) has its setting in France during World War I, uses Holy Week as a structural device, and has unmistakable parallels to events in the life of Jesus. Critics have had field days examining the biblical allusions in these and other Faulkner stories.

Clearly, the allusions are present in Faulkner's work in abundance, and they join references to a vast amount of literature other than the Bible. The question for the reader, of course, has to do with how these allusions are to be interpreted. What are we to make of consistent Christian references in the fiction of an outstanding American writer who, through at least a part of his career, was thought to be an apostle of despair and degradation? In this chapter, after looking briefly at Faulkner's use of Christ imagery in *Light in August* and *A Fable*, we will study more closely one of his short stories, "Uncle Willy."

As we might expect, Faulkner was asked many times in his later years about his use of Christian imagery. His answers were consistent. He talked about Christianity as a part of his background, and he talked about Christian images as tools for the development of his stories. On one occasion he said,

> Remember, the writer must write out of his background. He must write out of what he knows and the Christian legend is part of any Christian's background, especially the background of a country boy, a Southern country boy. My life passed, my childhood, in a very small Mississippi town, and that was a part of my background. I grew up with that. I

assimilated that, took that in without even knowing it. It's just there. It
has nothing to do with how much of it I might believe or disbelieve—it's
just there.[1]

Another time, he was asked if he intended Joe Christmas as a bearer of
Christ symbolism:

No, that's a matter of reaching into the lumber room to get out something which seems to the writer the most effective way to tell what he is
trying to tell. And that comes back to the notion that there are so few
plots to use that sooner or later any writer is going to use something that
has been used. And that Christ story is one of the best stories that man
has invented, assuming that he did invent that story, and of course it will
recur. Everyone that has had the story of Christ and the Passion as a part
of his Christian background will in time draw from that. There was no
deliberate intent to repeat it. That the people come first. The symbolism
comes second.[2]

These two quotations illustrate the way Faulkner tried to deal with
this issue. You may be disturbed at some of the things Faulkner says—
his use of the word "legend," the line about the relative unimportance
of his own belief or disbelief, or the suggestion that the Christ story
might be a human invention. For the moment, at least, try to pass over
these points: these comments were, after all, tape-recorded and so
were not finely tuned; and they are the words of a storyteller talking
about writing, not those of a theologian formulating doctrine. The
central emphases in Faulkner's answers seem to be that the writer
must work from his or her own experiences and that, in a culture
dominated by Christianity, Christian images may be useful devices for
the telling of a story.

What might we make of Faulkner's own Christian references? Can
we tell, as we study specific stories, why he uses biblical material in
them and how he uses it? Is his use completely casual, as his remarks
might suggest, or does there seem to be some reason behind the
allusions? Might an understanding of Faulkner's practice help us in
reading other literature? How are we to relate what Faulkner says he is
doing with what appears in the fiction itself?

It is impossible to know how many people today read Faulkner out
of pure pleasure rather than out of necessity (that is, having been
assigned to read a novel or short story in high school or college); nor
could we know how many who read this volume might be Faulkner
fans. The number, in either case, would be fairly small. So why drag
out a writer whose reputation was made way back in the 1920s and
1930s? Why not talk instead about a really up-to-date bestselling
novelist, a Herman Wouk or a Colleen McCullough? The reason for

the selection of Faulkner here is that his richness and depth still deserve our attention and will continue to do so after many a bestseller is forgotten: Faulkner is a great storyteller, a careful observer, a skilled writer, a person who knows some things about what makes human beings tick—and he is so much more. Faulkner wrote about people and about the motion of life.[3] He wrote about the problems, the complexities, the sorrows and pains, the joys, the laughter, the pure fun of living. We don't read Faulkner today just for some neat philosophy about human endurance in the face of life's difficulties; we also read because he knew how to tell a story and the reading is enjoyable.

For present purposes, we also read for an example of a writer who used Christian images without any apparent attempt to proclaim the gospel or become a hidden theologian. Faulkner at once accepted as important many values that have been central to Christianity and, at the same time, criticized a Christianity debased by its development and practice in our culture.[4] The task in this chapter is not to pass any sort of judgment on Faulkner's own beliefs or his articulation of them: it is, rather, to look at some of his fiction, applying the principles of interpretation we have discussed and trying to see how and why Faulkner uses Christian images as he does. The focus will be on the stories themselves. We will examine the Christian allusions in order to illustrate how we might deal with some of the problems identified in part 1, and we will find as we do so that the narrative itself is of more significance than one or two of its elements. In other words, the purpose of reading a story—by Faulkner or anyone else—is much broader than the tracing or interpreting of allusions, though that exercise will contribute to our general benefit from the story.

JOE CHRISTMAS

Light in August, after fifty years, remains one of the most complex, one of the most widely discussed and highly praised of Faulkner's nineteen novels. Much too rich for easy summary, it demands close reading and rereading. This is not to discourage you from attempting it but to present it as a novel that will certainly repay your efforts. Its four major characters have stories that are sometimes independent of one another but are eventually intertwined; by his careful use of structure and point of view, Faulkner makes of their lives a single, complex story. To attempt a statement of theme would be to oversimplify and distort. The novel is about human alienation and desperation; it is about sacrifice and endurance and love; it is about religious fanaticism and racial discrimination—both in their most devastating forms; it is about American life in the 1930s; it is about the South and the past and the shaping powers of our experiences on our life stories. Above all, it is about people.

One of its people, one of its major characters, is Joe Christmas. Given his name when he was found on a doorstep on Christmas Eve, Joe spent his first five years in an orphanage, his next fourteen with a stern Presbyterian foster father, and then entered a "street which was to run for fifteen years" of wandering, gambling, working, despairing.[5] During the present time of the novel, Joe becomes the lover of Joana Burden, a spinster in her early forties; after he murders her, he is tracked down and imprisoned; he escapes, is tracked again and killed. Such a two-sentence summary of Joe's life may make the story seem more melodramatic and sensational than it really is, and such a summary certainly cannot convey the deep tragedy of Joe's life.

Because of his name, his discovery on Christmas Eve, and his death as a scapegoat of society, Joe Christmas has been described by critics as one of Faulkner's Christ figures. We have already witnessed Faulkner's own response to the question about Christ symbolism in Joe Christmas. Critics are not put off by such denials, however: one has listed some fifteen points of parallel between the life of Joe and the life of Jesus; another has proposed that the whole novel is written in specific parallel with the Gospel of John.[6] Clearly, the name, if nothing else, does send some signals. Why would Faulkner use such a name if he intended no great symbolic meaning?

Perhaps this is the place to sharpen the distinction between allusion and symbol. The name of Joe Christmas is an allusion: it suggests for the reader, at the very least, the cultural holiday of Christmas and, at most, the birth of Jesus. Faulkner's use of the name to evoke those memories does not turn the character into a Christ figure. For Joe to be a symbol of Christ, the allusions would have to accumulate; they would have to build a consistent parallel to the story of Jesus so that Joe, in some sense, would be a modern reenactment of the ancient story. Faulkner says that is not what he is doing; but even if he were misleading his questioner or somehow mistaken about his own work, the novel itself would show that Joe's story moves in quite another direction from the story of Jesus and that the parallels which might seem to exist are more incidental than substantial. The critic whose major aim in reading seems to be the finding of religious symbols will note the allusions, stretch a few points to strengthen a case, and come up with a symbol. Careful reading of a narrative calls for scrutiny of allusions and a strong resistance to stretching anything. In this case, the novel as a whole does not present Joe Christmas as a Christ figure: his is the tragic existence of a person who is hopelessly confused about his own identity and who experiences God's love only as the "faded and weathered letters on a last year's billboard *God loves me too*."[7] We have to consider the rest of the novel also, and when we do we recall the stories of three other major characters and a host of minor ones. The reader will analyze the characteristics of Lena Grove, Byron Bunch, and Gail Hightower and will see how their stories meet the story of Joe Christmas to form the single, complex narrative of *Light in August*.

We may still ask, of course, how Faulkner uses the allusion in Joe's name. If we take seriously what Faulkner says about using Christian imagery as a tool in the development of his characters, then we have to wonder how the name of Joe Christmas works and in what sense it is such a tool. A part of the answer may lie in the obvious contrast between, on the one hand, the celebration and festivity and gift-giving associated with that holiday, even in secular observance, and, on the other, the lonely, tormented existence of a man who through most of his life has little to celebrate and experiences difficulty receiving or giving gifts. The irony of his name stays with us throughout the novel. Perhaps also by means of Joe's name and other allusions to Christian categories, Faulkner manages to keep the positive value of the Christ story constantly before the reader, reminding the reader of this distance between that ancient story and this modern one and presenting a norm against which the reader might judge the distorted religiosity of the characters in the novel. This is not to say that all readers have positive impressions about the Christ story or that Faulkner endorses all Christian values; rather, Faulkner recognizes the existence of those values, knows that some of his readers will respond to them, and so enriches his story by allowing the Christian references to bring depth to the reading—in the same way that he allows references to Buddha or, for that matter, Tennyson and Shakespeare, to add depth. For Faulkner, ultimately, the people are important, and the allusions add to the reader's perception of the characters.

THE CORPORAL

In *A Fable*, Faulkner is much more direct with his parallels to the story of Jesus, and the reader has another kind of problem. Faulkner acknowledged that he had tried in *A Fable* to retell "one of the oldest and most moving tragic stories of all," that of "the father who is compelled to choose between the sacrifice or saving of his son."[8] If he had said nothing at all in interviews about his intentions, we would not have been left in much doubt by our reading: the chapters of the novel are given the titles of days of the week, and their contents follow closely the events of the Holy Week of Jesus. The corporal and the twelve soldiers who are his followers enter the city of Paris in parade on Sunday, though they are prisoners; they have a Thursday night last supper together; a man named Judas betrays the corporal; another named Peter denies him; he faces a firing squad standing between two criminals and when he falls a curl of barbed wire forms a crown for his head; the three women who follow him are Marthe, Marya, and Magda; there is a form of resurrection.

In this case, we have a conscious effort to develop a plot and characters that explicitly parallel the New Testament accounts. Again, the reader will ask why Faulkner would do this. Faulkner's answer has another dimension besides the retelling of the tragic story of father-and-son conflict. He also said that he had wondered,

> Who might be in the tomb of the Unknown Soldier? And if that had been, if Christ had appeared again in 1914–15, he would have been crucified again. To tell that story, the thought was if I could just tell this in such a powerful way that people will read it and say this must not happen again, that is, if Providence, Deity, call Him what you will, had tried to save this world once, save men once by the sacrifice of His Son, that failed, He tried it again and that failed, maybe He wouldn't try it the third time, and so we must take warning because He may not try to save us again that way. Though that was incidental, I was primarily telling what to me was a tragic story, of the father who had to choose between the sacrifice or the saving of his son.[9]

Once again, Faulkner used Christian references to tell a story about people. One of the differences between his practice here and that in *Light in August* is that in *Light in August* he made occasional allusions to the Christ story, whereas in *A Fable* he multiplied parallels and intentionally structured the novel around the events in the life of Christ. Even if we understand that he wanted to tell his tragic story and that he was toying with the idea of Christ appearing a second time, we must still ask what he gained—or lost—by using the Christian background for *A Fable*.

When we read the book with care, we note that Faulkner also develops parallels to Christ outside the figure of the corporal, that there are numerous other New Testament references in the novel, and that there are significant differences between Faulkner's narrative and the account of the gospels.[10] These observations can lead us to conclude that Faulkner's point is not a rigid development of the corporal into a Christ figure but the use, again, of the Christ story and its values—values that are close to Faulkner's own list of human verities, the basic human truths of courage, honor, pity, and compassion. Christian references throughout the novel call attention to such values, to the possibility of human sacrifice for the sake of other persons, and to the hope that humanity will prevail in the face of all the difficulties of human existence. The task as one examines these references is not so much to evaluate Faulkner's theology or his own comprehension of the story of Jesus; it is, rather, to note the way his accumulated allusions are used to develop the plot and characters and to underscore his own world views.

WILLY CHRISTIAN

The short story "Uncle Willy," which first appeared in the *American Mercury* in 1935, presents us with yet another variation on Faulkner's use of Christian references. The fourteen-year-old narrator tells about Uncle Willy Christian, the bachelor who ran one of the drug stores in Jefferson, Mississippi, and was especially kind to the young boys on the sandlot baseball teams, treating them to ice cream cones after the games, giving the winning teams a prize, and letting them all watch him go behind his prescription counter, take out his "alcohol stove and fill the needle," and shoot "dope" into his arm.[11] Uncle Willy would go to Sunday school with the boys, sit quietly in their class, and then lead them back to the drug store to watch his Sunday shot. The boys enjoyed their attention from Uncle Willy until the preacher and a zealous lady from the church cured Uncle Willy of his habit. The narrator tells the amusing history of Uncle Willy's effort to get at his drugs, his absence for the cure and his return to town as an alcoholic, his second return with a wife from Memphis, his third return with an airplane, his spirited attempt to learn to fly, and his death in a plane crash. The story is funny, despite the death and the serious problems of drugs and alcohol, because Uncle Willy is a believable character in his resistance to reform, because the other adults are seen through the child's eyes and become ridiculous stereotypes, and because the narrator brings a special perspective to the story. Beyond the humor, though, is the significant and earnest difficulty of the young boy who tells the tale and finds himself in conflict with his father and the other adults, the boy who admires Uncle Willy and wishes he could explain to them his admiration for Uncle Willy and why he had seemed to help Uncle Willy go to his death in that airplane.

A community of readers could interpret this story from a variety of angles. They could examine Faulkner's use of the fourteen-year-old narrator, his development of the stereotypical preacher and female reformer, his portrayal of the black people in the story, and his handling of humor. In the relatively few studies of the story, critics have discussed Faulkner's development of narrative distance by having the boy tell the story, Faulkner's treatment of respectability by playing the bad influence of Uncle Willy against the perhaps equally bad influence of the preacher and church woman, and Faulkner's portrait of a carefree adult existence told as a childhood fable.[12] Readers will want to see if there is a balance between the seriousness of the narrator—who begins his story, "I know what they said. They said I didn't run away from home but that I was tolled away by a crazy man who, if I hadn't killed him first, would have killed me inside another week"[13]—and the humorous situations: Uncle Willy, being dried out and held in bed by his saviors, urging them, "Won't you please quit? Won't you please go away? Won't you please go to hell and just let me come on at my own gait?"[14] Readers may study the story to see if the narrator is to be believed at all. Are the adults right that he was lured away by an irresponsible and crazy old man, or is the boy right that he consciously helped Uncle Willy because he admired the man and wanted him free of those adults who would have destroyed him on their terms? Indeed, readers will search the story to see if they can answer those questions or if Faulkner has left them with ambiguity.

For the moment, look at the story from still another angle. We have been talking, in this chapter, about Faulkner's use of Christian images, and we have found not only that he made frequent reference to biblical material but that he also specifically drew upon the Christ story as a source of positive values for the telling of his stories. In "Uncle Willy" we find two interesting developments. One is that the character named Willy Christian does not seem, on the face of it, to lead a very "Christian" life, with his interests in drugs, alcohol, sex, and finally a suicidal obsession with flying an airplane. At the same time, Uncle Willy is in some ways a most genuine, believable, even likable human being, attentive to the children as other adults are not, even childlike himself, as Jesus said we should be to know the joys of God's love. The second development of interest to us now in the story is that the other adults, especially the Reverend Mr. Schultz and Mrs. Merridew the reformer, are from all outward appearances responsible, believing, energetic "Christians" who come across as obnoxious hypocrites. That is the way the narrator sees them, of course, and the narrator can be mistaken. After all, as some critics have noted, Uncle Willy was not a very good influence on young boys, and most people would prefer not to have their children associate with a drug-addicted, alcoholic, womanizing, crazy old man.[15]

Just at this point lies part of the interest and the irony of the story. In a sense, the adults are "right" in trying to rescue Uncle Willy from his addiction and, in the process, rescue their children from a dangerous influence; yet from the boy's point of view, they are needlessly cruel in robbing a gentle and kind man of his few pleasures in life. Uncle Willy is wrong to use the boys as his accomplices in getting alcohol and in lying to his sister, but it is to his credit that never—so far as the narrator tells us—does he give the slightest invitation to the boys to join him in his vices. And after he has been "saved" from drugs and drink, his escape from an institution and his frantic but futile efforts to fly an airplane seem one last and perhaps relatively healthy experience of human existence. Faulkner has said that there was something "almost immoral" about the way some people took to flying in those early days of the airplane, as though they were "outside the range ... not only of respectability, of love, but of God too"[16] (Faulkner himself enjoyed flying). Yet there is an exhilarating dimension to Uncle Willy's attempt at flight:

> and at night in the tent Uncle Willy's eyes would still be shining and he would be too excited to stop talking and go to sleep and I don't believe he even remembered that he had not taken a drink since he first thought about buying the airplane.[17]

So Faulkner leaves the reader feeling ambivalent at the end of this story, recognizing the proper, responsible role of the adults, sensing that Uncle Willy has finally found some purpose and enjoyment from life, and wondering about the effect of the whole experience on the young narrator. A good story about real people will often leave us just as puzzled as we sometimes are in our own lives.

But why does Faulkner use the name "Christian" here? Part of the reason would be to set up the contrasts and ironies we have been talking about in the preceding paragraph. Faulkner said, on occasion, that he had little use for organized religion, and in the characterizations of the Reverend Mr. Schultz and Mrs. Merridew he levels an attack on the self-righteousness that sometimes appears in the church. By applying the name "Christian" to Uncle Willy, Faulkner at least causes the reader to consider who in the narrative is really the Christian or what it might mean to be a Christian. In Japan, when he was asked about his belief in Christianity, Faulkner said, "I think that the trouble with Christianity is that we've never tried it yet."[18] Maybe this story suggests that a kind and honest man who cared about young children and spent time with them might be a better Christian than people who try to impose their own moral standards on others and are proud to call themselves Christians. Part of Faulkner's greatness, though, is that he does not allow this to be a cheap attack, the kind of trite blast against hypocrisy we often read in novels or see on our screens; rather, he deepens the issue by letting the reader recognize that the young narrator may be misjudging his elders.

A final and even tougher question is this: What is the reader who happens to be a Christian supposed to make of Faulkner's allusion in this story? First, the name of Uncle Willy is not the central issue of the story, so it would be sad for readers to get stuck there. Readers who are Christians may well get too much involved in fairly narrow issues that are of interest to them but that are incidental to the main thrust of the narrative. By raising the point of Faulkner's use of Christian references, I may myself have led us into just that trap; but it should be clear by now that we cannot approach a story simply through its explicitly religious material and that there is more in "Uncle Willy" than the character's last name. If you are talking about this story in a group, try to get beyond the simple Christian reference to more substantive issues about the credibility of the narrator, the ambiguity of Faulkner's approach, or the quality of life expressed by the different characters.

Second, Faulkner's own interpretation of Christianity is not the reader's concern. A theologically alert reader may conclude that Faulkner himself has a kind of moralistic understanding of Christianity, but Faulkner's position is really beside the point as we try to interpret the story. The reader deals with the people in the story as they are presented in the language and events of the narrative. Faulkner's comments about Christianity and his relationship to Christianity may be helpful to us as we try to understand him and his fiction, but we are not in the business of passing judgment about his opinions or faulting him for not being as sophisticated theologically as we might think we are ourselves. As we interpret the story, it is, first and last, the story itself we struggle with and read and analyze.

Third, we bring to the reading our own personal backgrounds, and the images of a story may set us off in directions of our own. The extensions of our imaginations and the development of our thought patterns as we leave the story are legitimate and valuable. We may think, for example, that in some sense Willy Christian is a pretty good image of what we estimate a Christian to be: at once trapped in self-indulgences and at the same time genuine, excited, kind—in our older language, sinner and saint simultaneously. When we move to such a thought, however, we have left the story; or we might say that the story has served as a launching pad for other ideas. It would be faulty interpretation to argue that Faulkner understood human nature in precisely those reformed, Christian terms; it is appropriate, however, to let the mind wander and let the story prompt other reflections.

William Faulkner is *the* major Southern writer, a touchstone for other authors, and a curse for all storytellers who come after him and have to endure comparison with him. He grew up in the South at a time when Christianity dominated the culture, when many, many people in the South went to church, read their Bibles, and knew the language and experiences of Christianity, whether they believed any of it very deeply or not. Perhaps even then, in the first decades of this century, the distance between popular faith and the New Testament witness was greater than anyone then felt it to be. At any rate, even though Faulkner wrote about and from a kind of Christian culture (or perhaps we should say a "cultural Christianity"), he also knew and wrote about people who had trouble believing and were either untouched by or, in some instances, damaged by that religious expression. Within just a few generations that hint of cultural unity would no longer exist, not at any depth, not for such numbers of people. Writers in the South would be left, even more so than Faulkner was, with inheritances and traditions, on the one side, and an increasingly modern world on the other.

7

FLANNERY O'CONNOR
"PARKER'S BACK"

In the fiction of Flannery O'Connor, we find fascinating sto-ries—and some problems. Flannery O'Connor was a writer who made no secret of her own faith or of her attempts to express that faith in her stories: "I shall have to speak, without apology, of the Church, even when the Church is absent; of Christ, even when Christ is not recog-nized."[1] Speaking generally of the Catholic writer, she said that inso-far as such a person "has the mind of the Church," he or she "will feel life from the standpoint of the central Christian mystery: that it has, for all its horror, been found by God to be worth dying for."[2] That perspective does not narrow but rather enlarges the writer's "field of vision." Her stance is a problem in terms of the issues we have been discussing about the interpretation of literature. What does the reader do with a writer who announces so forthrightly her intentions? Are we left only with propaganda? What happens to the objectivity of the text? Is the reader who is a Christian finally helped or hindered when the writer who is a Christian offers her own interpretations of her stories?

Flannery O'Connor lived most of her life in Milledgeville, Georgia, as a devout Roman Catholic, a skilled writer, and a person of deep humanity, faith, and humor. She studied writing and received a Mas-ter's degree at the University of Iowa; she spent some months writing in New York and Connecticut and returned to Milledgeville in 1950 when she was found to have the deadly disease lupus. Until her death in 1964 she lived with her mother on the family farm near Milledgeville, completing two short novels and two collections of short stories, the second one published posthumously. Her letters, which appeared in 1979 under the title *The Habit of Being*, reveal the quality of her life, her sense of humor, her continuing interest in the peafowls she raised, her broad reading, her faith, and her courage and lack of self-pity. Though her literary production was relatively small, she is widely recognized as one of the most important Southern writers of the past half-century and one who made a significant contribution to our national literature.

Part of her value in this present study has to do with the way she understood Christianity, its relation to culture, and the function of the believing writer in that context. As we attempt to become a community of interpretation in the modern world, at once believing God's story and listening to the stories around us, we do well to hear also the impressions of a sensitive artist who believed and listened and told her own stories. In a collection of her essays entitled *Mystery and Manners*, she talked about the world as a "territory held largely by the devil";[3] comments in the letters clarify what she meant. She wrote to one correspondent that the world of her day was going through a "dark night of the soul," a drastic loss of faith, and an inability to believe that God could exist; she said that the "very notion of God's existence is not emotionally satisfactory anymore for great numbers of people."[4] She was also frustrated that nobody in her audience, she felt, believed in the incarnation: "My audience," she wrote in 1955, "are the people who think God is dead."[5] In that context, then, she recognized that as a writer she would have trouble if she assumed her audience knew the language of faith as she knew it. An experience such as baptism, quite meaningful within a Christian community, is empty to the many people who live outside that community and are indifferent to it, if not offended by it. She said even "the word Christian is no longer reliable. It has come to mean anyone with a golden heart. And a golden heart would be a positive interference in the writing of fiction."[6]

Flannery O'Connor's response to such a cultural situation was to stand firm on her faith and try to break through the misunderstanding and indifference she saw in the culture. She knew the depth of the conflict: "That belief in Christ is to some a matter of life and death has been a stumbling block for readers who would prefer to think it a matter of no great consequence."[7] Because she evaluated the modern mind in this way, she consciously exaggerated in her fiction, in the hope of breaking through with deeper realities for people who are "not adequately equipped to believe anything."[8] She explained her method this way:

> When I write a novel in which the central action is a baptism, I am very well aware that for the majority of my readers, baptism is a meaningless rite, and so in my novel I have to see that this baptism carries enough awe

and mystery to jar the reader into some kind of emotional recognition of its significance. To this end I have to bend the whole novel—its language, its structure, its action. I have to make the reader feel, in his bones if nowhere else, that something is going on here that counts. Distortion in this case is an instrument; exaggeration has a purpose, and the whole structure of the story or novel has been made what it is because of belief. This is not the kind of distortion that destroys; it is the kind that reveals, or should reveal.[9]

Some readers have found this approach offensive, so that her attempt to express the gospel in fiction has been for them the same kind of stumbling block which the gospel itself is. Reading her interpretations and her statements of intention, the stories themselves may seem a little heavy-handed, as though they had been produced solely for the sake of the doctrinal point. And yet the stories are so good, the characters so real, O'Connor's perceptions so accurate, her language so specific and true that the reader is given at once a delight and a dilemma.

Will the stories themselves bear up under her interpretations? Should we read them only on her terms? Is she storyteller or proselytizer? This dilemma should not be allowed to block entirely the delight and enjoyment of reading her fiction.

"PARKER'S BACK"

"Parker's Back" is a fine story for examination, for several reasons. It contains explicit Christian references, and we are trying to learn how to handle those. It makes observations on several attitudes about Christianity as it exists in our society. It goes beyond allusion and reaches toward theological substance. Completed just a few months before her death, it was written at a time when she was probably at the peak of her writing powers. She had actually started on it in December 1960, and she knew then she had a special story: she said she was "having the best time I have had in a spell of working. If I can work it out, I'll have something here."[10] The next month she complained that the story was not "coming along too well. It is too funny to be as serious as it ought."[11] Then in June of 1964 she was trying from her hospital bed to finish it for the new collection of short stories; by July 11 she sent copies to friends for their advice, and though she was still "puttering" with it on July 21, by the 25th she had decided on "letting it lay."[12] She died on August 3, 1964.

Though the story itself is complex, its basic outline can be stated fairly easily. O. E. Parker, former sailor, present handyman, has in the course of his life covered his body with tattoos. In frustration over his relationship with his very religious wife, and after a rather shattering, revelatory experience, he decides to have his back, the last bare spot, covered with a picture of God—specifically, a stern Byzantine Christ from the tattooist's art book. After a brief time of being teased in a pool room and some self-examination regarding the figure on his back, he goes home where his wife fails to recognize the figure. When Parker explains, she charges him with idolatry, since God is a "spirit" in her view, and beats him on his back with a broom. Many features of the story deserve the reader's study; we will consider just a few scenes. This exercise should both demonstrate the analysis of a text and, at the same time, offer some help for interpretation of the story.

First, look at the episode that provides the initial dramatic break in the rather calm movement of the narrative. To this point in the story, we have observed Parker and his wife and have learned through flashbacks about his tattoos, their meeting and marriage. We have found that Sarah Ruth does not like her husband's tattoos and is warning him about God's judgment, and that Parker has been restless trying to think of some religious tattoo which Sarah Ruth might "not be able to resist."[13] Then, one day, as Parker is plowing a field, circling inward to a single old tree,

> his mind was on a suitable design for his back. The sun, the size of a golf ball, began to switch regularly from in front to behind him, but he appeared to see it both places as if he had eyes in the back of his head. All at once he saw the tree reaching out to grasp him. A ferocious thud propelled him into the air, and he heard himself yelling in an unbelievably loud voice, "GOD ABOVE!"
> He landed on his back while the tractor crashed upside down into the tree and burst into flame. The first thing Parker saw were his shoes quickly being eaten by the fire; one was caught under the tractor, the other was some distance away, burning by itself. He was not in them. He could feel the hot breath of the burning tree on his face. He scrambled backwards, still sitting, his eyes cavernous, and if he had known how to cross himself he would have done it. (p. 520)

Several things might strike the reader about this scene. Although in the story to this point the events have all been reasonable and believable, these lines contain hints that we are entering another dimension of reality. The first suggestion of a strange new development comes with the reference to the sun switching from his front to his back. Though that can be accounted for by his changing position on the tractor as he circles the tree, the wording suggests what Parker feels: that the sun is moving. Then there is Parker's sense of having eyes in the back of his head, and then his feeling that the tree is reaching out to grab him. Through these images, O'Connor gives the reader the idea that nature has suddenly come alive, that Parker is no longer the actor but is the receiver of some unusual activity. She intensifies this movement in the next paragraph as the tree catches on fire and the shoes burn apparently on their own. Then she intrudes, as the narrator, to be sure the reader has the same sense of this experience that Parker has: "If he had known how to cross himself he would have done it." There is some ambiguity in the line: is it that Parker thinks, "If I knew how to cross myself, I sure would do it," or is it that the narrator concludes, "Parker doesn't know how to cross himself and can't even think about that, but he has an experience of holiness such as people have when they are moved to cross themselves"? The narrator does not leave Parker's consciousness often, but on occasion she does. In either case, the reader senses with Parker the mysterious event. The burning tree and the castoff shoes have reminded some readers of the burning bush and the holy ground in Moses' story (Exod. 3:1–6). Parker's cry, "GOD ABOVE!" may suggest a curse or a revelation: the argument that he has been given a revelation is supported by Parker's movement directly to a tattooist to request a picture of God for his back. This passage works as a decisive turning point in the story, just as the experience is a turning point in Parker's life.

Before we examine more carefully a scene later in the story, we might recall two parts of the intervening account. Both these passages help us understand Parker's own reaction to the figure on his back. When the artist finally persuades Parker to look in the mirrors at his new tattoo, "Parker looked, turned white and moved away. The eyes in the reflected face continued to look at him—still, straight, all-demanding, enclosed in silence" (p. 526). Then, when the men in the pool hall see his back, their reaction leads Parker into a rage:

> "Maybe he's gone and got religion," some one yelled.
> "Not on your life," Parker said.
> "O. E.'s got religion and is witnessing for Jesus, ain't you, O. E.?"
>
> "What'd you do it for?" somebody asked.
> "For laughs," Parker said. "What's it to you?"
> "Why ain't you laughing then?" somebody yelled. Parker lunged into the midst of them and like a whirlwind on a summer's day there began a fight that raged amid overturned tables and swinging fists until two of them grabbed him and ran to the door with him and threw him out. Then a calm descended on the pool hall as nerve shattering as if the long barnlike room were the ship from which Jonah had been cast into the sea. (pp. 526–27)

These two scenes serve to show the reader that Parker is having to deal with the face on his back, almost unwittingly. The eyes seem to claim him. The tattoo challenges his self-understanding and threatens his life. What started out—in his mind at least—as an attempt to appease his wife has become a new reality, an inescapable command. "The eyes that were now forever on his back were eyes to be obeyed. He was as certain of it as he had ever been of anything" (p. 527). Whatever distresses he may now experience—wondering what Sarah Ruth will say, embarrassment with the men in the pool hall, tenderness and pain from the recent needlework—these passages make it clear that the figure on his back has forced him to a new examination of his life. Through these episodes Parker must come to terms with that figure; O'Connor uses them to let the reader also see the impact of the tattoo on Parker.

Look next at the scene of Parker's return to show his tattoo to Sarah Ruth. Late at night Parker knocks at the door, and Sarah Ruth pretends not to know him, not to know an O. E. Parker. Before they were married she had made him reveal the names behind those initials, but he never used those names and he forbade her to use them. Now she employs his secret against him:

> "Who's there?" the same unfeeling voice said.
> Parker turned his head as if he expected someone behind him to give him the answer. The sky had lightened slightly and there were two or three streaks of yellow floating above the horizon. Then as he stood there, a tree of light burst over the skyline. Parker fell back against the door as if he had been pinned there by a lance. (p. 528)

Once again, we see O'Connor using a description of the natural setting to move beyond the simple realism of the story and to evoke a sense of the supernatural. The movement of Parker's head and the narrator's use of "as if" hint at another presence; the burst of light (the tree reminding us of Parker's earlier encounter with a tree) has an effect on Parker deeper than we can immediately understand. Then, when Sarah Ruth asks again,

> Parker bent down and put his mouth near the stuffed keyhole. "Obadiah," he whispered and all at once he felt the light pouring through him, turning his spider web soul into a perfect arabesque of colors, a garden of trees and birds and beasts.
> "Obadiah Elihue!" he whispered. (p. 528)

Here the word "arabesque" will not only carry its own exotic connotations but will also remind the careful reader of O'Connor's use of the word earlier in the story. In describing Parker's campaign to ease his personal dissatisfactions by getting new tattoos, O'Connor portrays Parker as never having felt he had achieved the "one intricate arabesque of colors" that he remembered from the tattooed man at a fair; rather, the animals and birds on his body seemed to be living "inside him in a raging warfare" (p. 514). Now something has broken that warfare and brought a moment, at least, of peace, perhaps the first peace Parker has ever known. We are not told directly what causes his reaction, but the light pours through him just at the time he whispers his name. Obadiah means "worshipper of Yahweh" or "servant of Yahweh," and Elihue means "my God is he" or "God himself." We may doubt that Parker knew the Hebrew meanings of his name, but it is safe to guess that O'Connor did and that she used them intentionally. What happened to Parker may not even be understood at the time, but somehow the combination of his experience with the burning tree and his encounter with the figure on his back have now led him to a new sense of his own identity. Sarah Ruth forces him to say the name he does not want to say, but when he utters the words he feels brightness and perfection and harmony that he has not felt before.

What are we to make of the "new" Parker? One critic has said that "if anyone in modern literature becomes a Christ figure, Parker does."[14] Such a reading represents, in my view, both a misunderstanding of what a Christ figure is in literature and a faulty assessment of O'Connor's story. Parker is not a symbol of Christ: his life story bears no resemblance to the story of Jesus; his personality traits and language show no parallels. If Flannery O'Connor had wanted Parker to symbolize Christ, she of all writers knew how to have him do it. Parker may, on the other hand, represent the figure of a new disciple. The quality and depth of Parker's experience remain in some question, and I am convinced O'Connor purposely leaves it that way. The last we see of Parker, he is "leaning against the tree, crying like a baby" (p. 530), and interestingly enough the last we see of him is from Sarah Ruth's perspective. O'Connor does not allow us back into the consciousness of Parker at the end of the story, and the only hints of his feeling come from the word "stunned" in the next-to-last paragraph and his tears in the final one. Is he stunned and crying because what he thought would please Sarah Ruth not only fails but brings further abuse? Because he is overwhelmed by her attack? Because his new feeling of harmony has now been destroyed? Because his new faith has been rejected? Because the gospel is not understood in the modern world? We are left with many possibilities. I have tried to list some of them in an order ranging from the most obvious and natural to the most speculative and theological; in other words, there is more evidence in the story for my first supposition than for my last, though it may be that O'Connor's comments outside the fiction encourage the theological speculation.

Not only the final scene but other incidents of the narrative as well show that O'Connor concludes the story with some ambiguity. Readers eager to find their own theology or faith confirmed will jump to conclusions, but a cautious study indicates that O'Connor did not always spell out every message in bold print. Consider, for example, the imagery associated with Parker's feeling of transformation into a "perfect arabesque of colors." At that point in the story, when Parker whispers his name to Sarah Ruth, the "arabesque" is further pictured as a "garden of trees and birds and beasts" (p. 528). Some critics have taken that as an allusion to the image of the peaceable kingdom in Isa. 11:6 ("The wolf shall dwell with the lamb, and the leopard shall lie down with the kid"); they base their case on the contrast between the "perfect arabesque" that O'Connor describes here and the "haphazard and botched" quality of the tattoos on Parker's body during his time of dissatisfaction. In the earlier description, O'Connor had been more explicit in naming the animals: in first describing the tattoos, she had mentioned an eagle, a serpent, and a panther; when she talked about Parker's sense of internal warfare, she listed them again: "It was as if the panther and the lion and the serpents and the eagles and the hawks had penetrated his skin and lived inside him in a raging warfare" (p. 514). In an earlier draft of the scene in which he whispers his name and feels the "perfect arabesque," O'Connor had begun a description of a "garden of paradise where the panther and the lion and the serpent and the hawk . . ." and then had crossed out those words and written in "trees and birds and beasts." In other words, it seems she thought of putting in an explicit parallel to the Isaiah passage and then thought better of it, dropped the names of the animals, and by the final draft also abandoned the word "paradise," thereby making the allusion much less direct, Parker's new situation more ambiguous, and, I would argue, also making the story better.[15] The reader who knows Isaiah and remembers O'Connor's earlier reference to the animals at warfare within Parker may judge Parker's transformed life to be comparable to the peaceable kingdom that Isaiah promised, but O'Connor has certainly not demanded such an interpretation; indeed, she has backed away from it.

My own judgment is that Parker does represent a new disciple but in a rather sophisticated sense: that is, he is not the "convert" totally convinced and full of all the right theology, ready to serve and eager to evangelize; rather, he is the disciple who doesn't quite understand what has happened to him and isn't at all sure he likes it. You can't really say that Parker has made a firm decision for Christ. He has been claimed. This thing—whatever it is—has happened to him, and he will need some time to figure it all out. Whether or not he will do so would carry us beyond the story and into another kind of speculation. At any rate, such a portrait of the modern Christian is, in my mind, more realistic and believable, more true to my own experience, than are idealistic notions of contagiously enthusiastic followers.

In *The Identity of Jesus Christ*, theologian Hans W. Frei discusses, among other things, Christ figures in modern literature. He suggests that literary Christ figures often fail, at least from a theological point of view, because of the difficulty of substituting one specific savior for another, or of proposing universal savior figures. He suggests, further, that literary representations of disciples of Christ are often more successful and more helpful to believers, since the disciple figures allow for some distance from the Christ and do not alter the distinctiveness of the gospel story of Jesus. "It is the *disciple* who is believable, precisely because he follows Christ without trying to become Christ, at a distance rather than from too nearby, or with that intimacy of total contrast which is paradoxically one with total identity."[16] What this theologian has to say about Christ figures is more perceptive than what many literary critics have said. Frei allows that literary Christ figures may nonetheless be of some value to modern Christians, but he concludes that the "successful depiction of a disciple" may be more helpful than the "unsuccessful straining after a Christ figure."[17] Flannery O'Connor seemed to know that too, since she has many portraits of disciples and not one character whose life story closely parallels that of Jesus.

In the preceding discussion of "Parker's Back," I have looked closely at the text, at the actual words of the story, and I have tried not to let O'Connor's theological position influence me overmuch. Of course, I cannot forget what I have read in her letters and essays, just as I cannot close off my own background from my reading of her fiction. Perhaps a reader from outside the South and one with very little exposure to Christianity would interpret the story differently from the way I did. I would not argue that my reading is the only legitimate one, but I would encourage interpretation based on a close reading of the text and illumined, where that is helpful, by knowledge of the author's background and ideas, as well as by consciousness of the reader's own presuppositions and influences. In O'Connor's case, it may well be that we know too much about what she thought. Still, the stories themselves are complex and rich enough to warrant investigation. If you look at them carefully, you find that she doesn't spell everything out in unmistakable terms; rather, the puzzles of the narratives drive us back into the text to see if its words and images, its characters and plot developments, will help us solve the puzzles. To the degree that we cannot figure out a story without the author's interpretive comments, the story must be a failure—a noble failure, if it is true in O'Connor's case. But to the degree that a story engages our attention, compels scrutiny, makes connections in our minds with other ideas and so leads us beyond itself, and delights us along the way, it is well worth our time in both the reading of it and in discussion within a community of interpreters.

Flannery O'Connor's fiction offers many gifts. A community of readers who are Christians may have to approach her work with a double interest. On the one hand, we will read the stories and apply all the principles of literary criticism—analyzing style, characterization, allusion, structure, and other elements of fiction—just as we would with any other writer. Under this interest we will enjoy her as a storyteller, and we will likely sometimes be confused and sometimes enlightened, as we are with most good fiction. But, on the other hand, we will find another interest in her work as well, and perhaps the problem of reading her stories will become a bonus. Because she was a Christian and tried to express her faith in her fiction, we have a special invitation to let our imaginations roam around in her world and see where we are led.

Perhaps the story of "Parker's Back" works on one level for most readers in somewhat the following way: Parker has an extraordinary experience that holds the potential of leading him out of his anxious and dissatisfied life into a new kind of peace and harmony; his religious wife fails to understand his personal satisfaction, just as she fails to receive his gift to her, and he is left in tears by her response. Perhaps such an interpretation would come fairly easily to most readers. Readers in a Christian community, whether or not they know O'Connor's letters and essays, would find themselves of necessity going further. After all, it is a picture of Christ on Parker's back, and Parker is named Obadiah Elihue, and his final acknowledgment of that name does seem to make a difference to him. We would not be out of line, then, to consider what it might mean if Parker were O'Connor's representation of a modern disciple: someone who is somewhat confused by the role, rejected by the culture, and disappointed by that rejection, but who still feels that (for whatever reason, but certainly not from personal faith or effort or achievement) God cares and has brought a garden of wholeness and peace to a life that had felt like spider webs.

8

ERNEST J. GAINES
"A LONG DAY IN NOVEMBER"

Ernest J. Gaines has said that he came from people who were "tremendous storytellers."[1] His own novels and short stories show that he not only listened to his people but also became quite a storyteller himself. One catches from his work the distinctive language and vivid setting of the Louisiana plantation, the strong ties of family, church, and community. The clear and believable personalities of many characters ranging in age from six to one hundred and ten years and an awareness of the weaknesses and enduring strengths of humanity also come through. While he is probably best known through the television production of his novel *The Autobiography of Miss Jane Pittman* and his short story "The Sky Is Gray" (in the "American Short Story Series" on educational television), Gaines has also written four other novels, published a collection of short stories, and received considerable critical acclaim.

Born on a Louisiana plantation in 1933, Gaines has continually made that territory the setting of his fiction. Although he now lives in California where his family moved when he was a teenager, he returns to Louisiana about once a year and says he will probably write about his home country until "I get it all out of me" and "I hope I never do."[2] The United States Army claimed two years of his life, and his formal education after high school took place at San Francisco State College and Stanford University, but resources of his early years have established the subject for his writing. Gaines has reported that he was raised a Baptist, baptized at the age of twelve, and taught in local Catholic schools. He was cared for by his aunt, a woman who, despite severe physical handicaps, took care of all the household chores and demonstrated the courage, good humor, and strength that characterize many of the elderly women of Gaines's stories. The people and places of his home have been his subject, and the reader meets both impressive individuals and an influential community.

I

While we will concentrate here on one short story, the rest of Gaines's fiction certainly merits reading and more critical study than it has so far received. We cannot review all of his work here, but *The Autobiography of Miss Jane Pittman*[3] deserves notice, since Gaines received national attention through the televised version of that novel. Perhaps true readers are never quite satisfied with films made from literature, and we are likely to say consistently, "I enjoyed the book more." A decisive difference between the television program and the novel is worth mentioning here for two reasons: first, probably more people saw the show than read the book, and those viewers should be aware of some changes; second, the novel deals with storytelling and community in terms consistent with the discussion in part I of this volume.

Several critics of the television version have noted significant adjustments that, in their view, alter the thrust and power of the work.[4] The main direction of their criticism has been that the television production made the story more palatable to white viewers, more sentimental and safe, and more a portrait of a single, remarkable woman than a presentation of a courageous people. Many points of difference have been raised. A major one has to do with the television show's substitution of a white reporter for the novel's black history teacher as the person who hears and transmits the story of the 110-year-old former slave. One effect of that change is to make the story of Jane Pittman seem more like a human interest story, a fascinating feature article arising from the civil rights movement of the 1960s, whereas the novel conveys a century-long story of heroic people whose heroism does not simply come to life at the drinking fountain of a small Southern town's courthouse square but has been expressed and suffered through many generations. The television show, for all its problems, made a positive contribution to our common life by presenting a moving story of the black experience to a national audience. Still, people who saw the film would do well to read the novel also and consider the differences.

Consider this difference: the reporter in the film is interviewing an elderly woman who has been a stranger to him before this interview, and he is, essentially, getting her story; the history teacher in the novel is having repeated conversations with a woman he has known for years, one who has been recognized as protector, spokesperson, mother, and model to this community for generations past. Further, this history teacher knows that what Jane is telling him is not just Jane's story but is really the story of the whole people. In a sense, he is recording folk history; and when he is asked why he doesn't just let his students read the history books, he says it is because "Miss Jane is not in them."[5] At the end of the introduction, the history teacher-editor (the device Gaines uses to tell the story) thanks all the people who sat with Miss Jane as she talked and who filled in for her when she couldn't remember or got tired; he thanks them and acknowledges that all the loose ends cannot be tied "together in one neat direction." After all, he writes, "Miss Jane's story is all of their stories, and their stories are Miss Jane's."[6] For all its other interests, *The Autobiography of Miss Jane Pittman* provides an example of a community trying to understand its own story and, at least in part, becoming aware of the story and comprehending it through the retelling of it.

II

When we turn now to Gaines's rather lengthy short story "A Long Day in November," we find what appears to be a simple domestic tale, not dealing at all with racial conflict or political tensions. Printed first in Gaines's collection of stories entitled *Bloodline*,[7] this story presents an episode in the life of one small family in the plantation's quarters as that episode is seen through the eyes of a six-year-old boy. The basic action can be quickly summarized. Because his father has been spending too much time with his automobile, the boy's mother one morning takes the boy away from his home and his father and returns to her mother's house (where her mother encourages courting by another man). The father comes for his family, is run off by his wife's mother and a shotgun blast, and persuades the boy to follow him in an effort to find help—first from the preacher, and then from Madame Toussaint, the "hoo-doo woman" who tells him that if he wants his wife back he must set fire to his car. Reluctantly, the father follows her instructions, burns his car, wins back his wife, and begins to accept new levels of responsibility as husband and father. Through this simple plot, we also learn some things about a young boy facing early tests of independence, about causes of marital strife, about life among the cane cutters of a Louisiana plantation, and about the effectiveness of religion, superstition, and magic.

One of the beauties of the story is the way Gaines creates a distinctive tone through the use of such a young narrator. "A Long Day in November" gives us an opportunity to push a little further the discussion in part I about tone and point of view and to demonstrate how those elements of fiction operate in a particular story. In this case, it is the language of the six-year-old boy that helps create the atmosphere of the narrative. We see everything through his eyes, and we hear only what he hears, although we will be able to understand language, event, and implication that the little boy cannot grasp. The effect is to draw the readers into a special confidence of the author while creating sympathy between the readers and the young narrator. The simple sentences through which the child's thoughts are presented, the unadorned recording of the adults' conversations, the child's view of the adults' movements—all these contribute to the story's tone and help to convince us that it is a child's story.[8]

One technique by which Gaines manages to create a believable six-year-old narrator is the repetition of phrases. Note the way the repeated phrases in the opening paragraphs give us right away a strong impression of a child at the edge of sleep:

> Somebody is shaking me, but I don't want get up now, because I'm tired and I'm sleepy and I don't want get up now. It's warm under the cover here, but it's cold up there and I don't want get up now.
> "Sonny?" I hear.
> But I don't want get up, because it's cold up there. The cover is over my head and I'm under the sheet and the blanket and the quilt. It's warm under here and it's dark, because my eyes's shut. I keep my eyes shut because I don't want get up. (p. 3)

Thus, at the very beginning of the story we are given the pattern of short clauses, accumulated and often repeated, and we are immediately brought into the mind of the child and see the world as he sees it. That same simplicity and accumulation recurs throughout the narrative, whether we are following the child's dreams or watching the adults with him. These two paragraphs illustrate how Gaines encourages us to see what Sonny sees:

> Mama is frying salt meat in the skillet. The skillet's over one hole and the tea kettle's over the other one. The water's boiling and the tea kettle is whistling. I look at the steam shooting up to the loft.
>
> Daddy pours some water in the wash basin and washes his face, and then he washes my face. He dumps the water out the back door, and me and him sit at the table. Mama brings the food to the table. She stands over me till I get through saying my blessing, and then she goes back to the stove. Me and Daddy eat. (pp. 14–15)

That is the child's view: simple and direct. Even if we did not know from the preceding dialogue that the parents had been arguing, we certainly will sense here the isolation and independence of the two adults. The child does not explain even to himself that his parents are having trouble, but the form of the language and the content of the sentences will let the reader know that the child also feels the adults moving in two separate spheres.

Critics have discussed, and Gaines has acknowledged, the influence of Ernest Hemingway on his work.[9] Maybe it is easiest to see that influence in the passages just quoted: such short, simple clauses have usually been thought characteristic of Hemingway's style. Still, readers familiar with Hemingway will know, even on the basis of just the few sentences quoted above, that Gaines is using the short clauses here differently from the pattern in which Hemingway often used them. In this story, at least, it is clear that the accumulation of short clauses helps make the reader believe the story belongs to a six-year-old boy. Further, we can note that Gaines uses the short clauses—as indeed Hemingway sometimes does—to slow down the motion. This is partly because the sentences indicate continuing action ("frying," "boiling," "whistling," "shooting") and partly because they name, though very briefly, actions that take some time to accomplish (washing the face, saying the blessing, eating the meal).

One might think that such simple constructions and a narrative from the point of view of a child would severely limit the story and prohibit deep analysis of the story's exploration of human problems. It is true that Sonny is not able to articulate much criticism of the adults or make sophisticated observations about their behavior; these limitations are appropriate for a child his age. At the same time, however, we do know what the child is feeling. Early in the narrative, at one point, Sonny is lying in bed, and he begins thinking about their pig, Paul, outside in the cold, and Sonny thinks, "I'm sure glad I ain't a pig. They ain't got no mama and no daddy and no house" (p. 9). He thinks the same thing later as he watches birds: "No daddy, no mama—I'm glad I'm not a bird" (p. 38). Through Sonny's reflection, then, the reader is able to understand that the child does value his own home and wants his parents together. In the report of Sonny's difficulties at school—wetting his pants, dealing with the teasing of the other children, missing his lesson—we also recognize the effect of his parents' troubles on him. Gaines understates the problem but leaves the point unmistakable.

Another means of communicating more to the adult reader than a six-year-old might reasonably communicate is the straightforward recording of the conversations of the adults in the story.[10] Though the boy does not comprehend all that goes on around him, the story comes to us through his consciousness and works as if his eyes were a camera and his ears a tape recorder to transmit to us all that he sees and hears. Sonny is a keen observer, as we have already noticed, but he hears well also. Gaines is able to use Sonny's good eyes and ears to let us in on conversation and events that the child himself could not describe so clearly. For example, as they are on their way back from Madame Toussaint's house, Sonny's father is talking out loud, partly to Sonny, partly to himself, about what he should do with her suggestion that he burn up his car. Through Sonny's ears, we hear all his father says, hear him wonder why the only thing another of Madame Toussaint's customers "had to do was pop Julie on the butt little bit every night 'fore she went to sleep" while he was told to burn his car. "Now, that don't sound right, do it?" he asks Sonny (p. 63), who replies, as he has to other questions from his father, "Hanh?" Sonny also hears his mother say that "she didn't do her and Daddy's thing with Mr. Freddie Jackson," and he hears the "spring on Mama and Daddy's bed. I hear it plenty now," but we have no indication that he knows what any of those things mean. He does associate them with the security of his home, however, and so "feels good" when he crawls down to the warmth and darkness under his covers as his parents revive their relationship (p. 79). The reader knows more than the narrator because the words and actions have been reported even though the narrator did not understand them. The effect of this dramatic irony is to build our confidence in and attraction for Sonny and to contribute to the genuineness of the story.

III

Many other dimensions of this story merit discussion, but for now we will examine only the specifically "religious" material in the narrative and its overall meaning. On the surface at least, "A Long Day in November" does not seem to be a religious story at all. Certainly, if we compare it with the direct references to Christianity we have found in Faulkner and O'Connor, the story does not operate with such obvious allusion and implication. It is safe to say there are no Christ figures here and no overbearing symbolism. Rather, the religious material of the story seems perfectly natural and unpretentious: the people say their prayers at night, say a blessing over meals, call on their pastor when they are in trouble, and are involved in the life of their church. On one level the story suggests that such religious activity is a clear part of the life of those people; not to describe it or mention it as part of their daily routine and thought would be to describe their lives falsely. Religion to them is as natural as eating food, using a toilet, making love—all of which are part of this story.

On another level, Gaines offers some criticism of the way the church operates for these people. Two incidents in the narrative might imply such criticism. When Daddy is first turned away from his mother-in-law's house, he goes immediately to the preacher, and the preacher listens to the story. Although he has trouble believing that "Sister Rachel" would chase her son-in-law away with a shotgun and encourage adultery, he goes right then to talk with Sister Rachel. When the preacher has finished, he doesn't really offer much help to Sonny's father: the preacher tells him to "be strong" and counsels prayer and says he hopes "everything comes out all right" and that they just have to "leave it in God's hands." Sonny notices that the preacher "looks at me like he's feeling sorry for me," but he hears his father's complaint: "When you want one of them preachers to do something for you, they can't do a doggone thing. . . . Nothing but stand up in that church-house and preach 'bout Heaven" (p. 44). The second incident that might imply criticism of the church appears when Sonny's daddy talks to Mr. Johnny Green about the counsel Green had received from the voodoo woman. Madame Toussaint had told Green that his marital troubles had arisen because he had been spending too much time at the church; Mr. Johnny, who had been raised in a churchgoing family, decided to ask God about that, and God told him to follow Madame Toussaint's advice: "Slack up going to church. Go twice a week, but spend the rest of the time with her. Just like that He told me. And I'm doing exactly what He said" (p. 57). Now, in neither of these incidents is Gaines heavy-handed or sarcastic in his depiction of the church or the religious experience of the people. If the preacher is ineffectual from Daddy's perspective, he is nonetheless an influential person in the community, the first person Daddy turns to, and apparently a respected pastor for Sonny's mother and grandmother. Perhaps the point is that Gaines does not have an attack on religion as his primary purpose in telling the story.[11] He reports what is there in the daily life of the plantation and observes that excessive churchgoing by one spouse can be as damaging to a marriage as excessive attention to an automobile.

When we attempt to say what this story is about, we recognize that what seems to be a simple narrative has complex levels of meaning. Gaines himself has pointed out that the story serves a function as the introductory story in the *Bloodline* collection: the narrator in each of the succeeding stories is a little older—a boy of eight in "The Sky Is Gray," a young man of nineteen in the third story, and, finally, in the fifth story one of the central characters is the elderly, dying Aunt Fe. The narrators, in other words, each have increasingly broader ranges of vision, and that accounts, in part, for the confinement of the first story to the plantation setting.[12] Gaines has said that "A Long Day in November" is "like planting a grain and its sprouting" in relation to the other stories in *Bloodline*.[13] We would have to read and discuss the other stories in order to see clearly how this story relates to them, but it is evident that Gaines placed this story first intentionally and that he meant for there to be points of connection between the stories of the collection.

IV

As was noted back in part I, readers may have difficulty coming up with statements about a story's theme. Gaines has said that the father-son theme is important to him and that this story is partly about a father's search for his son.[14] Many critics have talked about "A Long Day in November" in terms of the theme of manhood.[15] That theme certainly appears in other stories and novels by Gaines; and here we see it, for example, in the words of Sister Rachel after Eddie has burned his car: "I just do declare. . . . I must be dreaming. He's a man after all" (p. 71). The importance of Eddie's manhood seems to account also for the beating that his wife demands from him after they have returned home: she asks for the beating so he won't be the "laughingstock of the plantation" for having burned up a three-hundred-dollar automobile in order to get his wife back (pp. 74–76). And to be sure, Eddie's coming to maturity and responsibility has its parallel in the experience of Sonny trying to learn his school lesson, avoid wetting his pants, and beat Billy Joe Martin at marbles.

One question a reader might ask in trying to arrive at the meaning of a story is whether or not the protagonist has changed in the course of the narrative. One critic has argued that Sonny does not change in this story, since at the end he is still under the warm covers of his bed and has not yet learned to be courageous.[16] If we compare the opening paragraphs with the closing paragraphs, we realize, of course, that images are repeated: Sonny is back in the warm bed at the end of the narrative, and he likes it because it is dark and warm (p. 79). Test your own reading. It seems to me that Sonny is a little better off at the end of this long day than he was at its dawn. He is still a six-year-old, of course, and we cannot expect too much courage from him, but his home now seems to be in order, he has his homework prepared, his father is going to school with him to talk with his teacher (for the first time ever), and Sonny at least feels that he can face his friends and even defeat Billy Joe in marbles and in running. No doubt Sonny will face difficult days ahead; lasting changes in personal development do not occur overnight. Still, his environment is different, and there are signs that the family may know more stability than it has in the past: within that new climate, Sonny seems to experience growth appropriate to a six-year-old in this one significant day. We need not make too much of this change, but perhaps part of the story's meaning is that a child's sense of well-being and potential for development to maturity and health have a great deal to do with the stability of the home and the relationship of the parents. That is no astounding observation, but it may well strike us afresh as we live through the day with these quite believable people.

The story prompts one final note. Most readers will recognize the legitimacy of Madame Toussaint's advice: Eddie has been spending too much time with his car—driving around, playing mechanic—and not enough with his wife and son. The car has become a toy, an idol. The voodoo woman knows that he has to get rid of the car completely, has to destroy the idol and make a radical change, if he wants to live with his wife. In a way, this is the common-sense advice of Jesus that no one person can serve two separate and competing authorities. Gaines may not have thought of the biblical passage (Matthew 6:24), and the story is not likely to be an enactment of that passage. On the contrary, the advice, in the context of the story, is commonplace and fairly self-evident: it comes from the voodoo woman, not the preacher, and it is, in a sense, good secular counsel.

The advice is worth some special notice here, however, since it may carry additional meaning for the reader who is a Christian. Theologian Paul Tillich has described faith as "ultimate concern," observing that we all have many concerns in our lives and that some of those concerns will claim, or attempt to claim, every ounce of our energy and every moment of our time. When some one concern claims to be the most important of all our interests, it demands in effect that we surrender our lives to it, even if we have to reject all other interests or subordinate them to that ultimate one.[17] Every person has ultimate concerns; every person puts faith in something. For the Christian, God is the "ultimate concern" who claims our attention above all other claims; we live by God's love and through our confidence in that love—not through our confidence in making money, having a position, owning a car, or even going to church. Now, this is not to suggest that Gaines has read Tillich and is trying to express Tillich's definition of faith in this short story; that is not at all the point. The story itself does not suggest any direct connection between what Gaines wrote and what Tillich wrote. The story does present an idea that is similar, and the reader who knows Tillich, or for that matter the reader who recalls Jesus' words about serving two authorities or the commandment to have no other gods, may well bring them to mind on hearing Madame Toussaint's advice. It isn't that Gaines had all that in mind. It is, rather, that our imaginations work to carry us from the image before us to our previous experiences, and in that way a simple story reminds us of what we have understood about faith.

Ernest J. Gaines's story "A Long Day in November" holds interest for its readers on a number of levels. Whatever response it may evoke, it does not seem primarily to be a story loaded with complex religious allusions and symbols, nor with social commentary, nor with racial bitterness or directives, nor with psychological profundities. Perhaps a little of each of these ingredients may be found, but the story seems more the telling by a small boy about an important day in his life, the day his father accepted family responsibilities, the day he himself began to believe he might also grow up and be able to stand, loved and confident. In this examination of the story, we have seen that part of its richness comes from Gaines's skillful presentation of the point of view, his careful style, and his exact use of words. Whether or not the story indirectly relates to any of our experiences of faith—and since that is not its major purpose, it may well not make those connections—it has its own beauties and powers which we can enjoy again and again. It is a good example of a story which operates without mystery or subtlety to help us understand ourselves and our society and to recall for us some basic human values.

9

ALICE WALKER
"THE WELCOME TABLE"

"What the black Southern writer inherits as a natural right is a sense of *community*," wrote Alice Walker in 1970.[1] We have seen that Gaines certainly develops his fiction from such a "sense of community," and though we did not talk about it specifically in the chapter on Faulkner, those who know his fiction know that he received this particular inheritance as well and demonstrated in story after story the importance of community among blacks and whites—separately and together—in the South. From the perspective of the black writer, however, the sense of Southern community remains dramatically distinctive from that of the white Southern writer: a white writer may feel that blacks and whites belong to a Southern society; the black writer knows that the Southern community has never been inclusive, and that an exclusive black community has been a necessary fortress against white prejudice and hatred. Relationships within each community, as well as between them, have been extremely complex and make discussion of community in the South difficult at best. Most generalizations, to be sure, will fall flat. Alice Walker is an accomplished artist who knows the South and recognizes many of life's complexities.

I

Although, like Gaines, Alice Walker now lives in California, the South is her home and the setting for her poetry and fiction. She was the eighth child born to sharecropping parents in 1944 in Eatonton, Georgia (which was also the home of Joel Chandler Harris, the Southern writer who created the Uncle Remus tales). Alice Walker attended Spelman College in Atlanta and then Sarah Lawrence in New York, traveled in Africa, was a caseworker in New York City and a civil rights worker in the South, and in recent years has been associated with several colleges and universities as a writer in-residence. Her first book of poetry, *Once,* appeared in 1968, and her first novel, *The Third Life of Grange Copeland,* was published in 1970. Since then she has published essays, poetry, and stories, as well as a second novel, *Meridian,* in 1976 and in 1982 *The Color Purple,* for which she received a Pulitzer Prize in literature.

Like Flannery O'Connor, Alice Walker knows why she writes. The reasons are different from O'Connor's, but they are in some ways just as penetrating and serious. She has stated some of those reasons, and perhaps they should be clear from the outset. She said in an interview, "I am preoccupied with spiritual survival, the survival *whole* of my people," and I am "committed to exploring the oppressions, the insanities, the loyalties, and the triumphs of black women."[2] That she brings to her writing such an agenda does not necessarily make her a propagandist; the work itself determines that judgment, and the work holds up quite well. Because Walker wants to write about the survival of her people and about the oppressions and triumphs of black women, some readers may be immediately turned away from her stories, and others may find a quick and easy affinity with them. She is a good enough writer to help those who are offended begin to understand another perspective, and she can lead those with easy affinity to new self-awareness.

Though we might not have guessed it on first reflection, Alice Walker has reason to like Flannery O'Connor. They had some things in common: strong mothers, commitment to a vision, skill at writing, and not least, growing up only a few miles (and twenty years) apart in middle Georgia. She likes O'Connor partly because of the way O'Connor could write about women, the South, even blacks, without myth, without sentiment, without nonsense. In an essay, Walker says she liked especially O'Connor's portraits of Southern white women

> because when she set her pen to them not a whiff of magnolia hovered in the air (and the tree itself might never have been planted), and yes, I could say, yes, these white folks without the magnolia (who are indifferent to the tree's existence), and these black folks without melons and superior racial patience, these are like Southerners that I know.[3]

Flannery O'Connor could live in the South and write about the South without propagating old Southern myths and dragging up Southern sentiment: "She was for me," Walker says, "the first great modern writer from the South."[4] O'Connor and Walker did not hold a common faith, but they did share a commitment about writing, a seriousness of intention, and a certain realism about their setting and their people.

Before we examine one of Walker's stories, we can say more about her commitments, not in order to demonstrate how the commitments are worked out in the fiction—indeed, we could read the fiction without any knowledge whatsoever of the writer's personal persuasions—but in order to observe the similarities and contrasts between Walker and O'Connor, whose commitments we have already discussed. We have noted the intensity of O'Connor's Christian conviction, and we have seen the problems and the opportunities such conviction can present to the reader of her stories. While Walker talks a great deal in her poetry and fiction about God, spirituality, and the church, her perceptions are not at all O'Connor's perceptions. About God, Walker says, "I don't believe there is a God, although I would like to believe it. Certainly I don't believe there is a God beyond nature. The world is God, Man is God. So is a leaf or a snake."[5] O'Connor would have been horrified at such an Emersonian notion, and she may have been less patient with Walker's pantheism (if that's what it is) than Walker has been of O'Connor's Catholicism—though O'Connor's letters do show her to be quite tolerant of people struggling with belief. Walker says that she rejected the Christianity of her parents and that only later did she realize "they had been force-fed a white man's palliative, in the form of religion" and they had "made it into something at once simple and noble."[6]

Yet at the same time, Walker has an abiding confidence in the human spirit, its capacities, its creativity, and its strength. She sees that spirit expressed especially in black women:

> For these grandmothers and mothers of ours were not Saints, but Artists; driven to a numb and blinding madness by the springs of creativity in them for which there was no release. They were Creators, who lived lives of spiritual waste, because they were so rich in spirituality—which is the basis of Art—that the strain of enduring their unused and unwanted talent drove them insane.[7]

These women handled their creativity by expressing it in other ways— her own mother and many others, for instance, by planting and caring for gardens and so "ordering the universe in the image of her personal conception of Beauty."[8] Because she sees this creativity and strength, Alice Walker has hope for humanity, and many of her stories turn on the new opportunity for fulfillment and contribution by black women today.[9]

Alice Walker is a feminist—or as she prefers to say, a "womanist"[10]—but she is not strident, and her literature has its own integrity and quality. She cares deeply about women, the indignities they have suffered, and the potential they have before them, and her portraits of them show her concern and her intimate knowledge. But her range of vision is broad and she also manages objectivity, realism, and humor. Part of literature's task is to enable readers to see from new angles and to experience realities other than their own, or to know their own more deeply. Many readers—black and white, male and female—may feel some shock in reading Walker, but that can become a shock of recognition, and then the literature begins to work. The shock comes not because her voice is strident but because the stories ring true.[11]

The nature of her commitment can be seen clearly in her poetry. While this is not the place for discussion of the poems, a brief reference to them will underscore what has been said about her major themes. Those themes stand out especially in the 1973 collection entitled *Revolutionary Petunias and Other Poems*.[12] Some of these poems grew from her experiences with the civil rights movement; others stem from memories of her childhood and the people who nurtured her. From them all the reader gets to know the "sense of community" that Walker regards as the inheritance of the black Southern writer. She recalls the relatives who were important to her upbringing, and she recalls the church as part of her own history. One dominant image is of strong, older women who saw to it that the children made it to church services and who did the teaching and the encouraging. Walker suggests that the doctrine she learned in those days was not, in the long run, nearly so important to her as the dialogue and the support given especially by the women around her. If she can no longer believe the concepts that were vital to Flannery O'Connor's commitment, Alice Walker still remembers the value of the community and the strength of the women and men who taught and directed and supported her. The poems reveal a sense of humor, an appreciation of the past, a love of life, an honor for women, a way of finding personal identity through participation in a particular community: all these mark Walker's fiction and form the background out of which she writes.

II

"The Welcome Table," from the 1973 collection *In Love & Trouble: Stories of Black Women*, is by far the shortest of the stories we are studying.[13] More a sketch or vignette than a short story, it tells of an old black woman taking a seat in a country church on a Sunday morning, ignoring requests that she leave, being carried out of the church, and then walking down the highway where she meets and talks with Jesus; later, she is found dead on the roadside.

For all its brevity, though, the reader senses a compact power, an explosiveness almost, and at the same time, tenderness, irony, humor, mystery. The plot is simple, character development limited, social commentary rather obvious, and its seven pages of print are like the visible part of a plant with a deep root system. Because the story is so short, we can look at several different elements, trying to see what its questions are and how Walker makes it work.

The story has three sections, with a double space between paragraphs marking the points of division. The first seven paragraphs are told from the point of view of the members of the church, although they themselves are being observed by a narrator who sees the irony of the whole situation; this first section moves from the arrival of the black woman to her expulsion from the church. The second section, three paragraphs, is told from the point of view of the old woman and describes her walk with Jesus. The final paragraph comes from a somewhat detached, almost impartial narrator who knows the minds of the black and the white communities but claims no special knowledge of the event itself; through this narrator we learn of the woman's death and the reactions to it. Part of Walker's accomplishment in the story comes through her use of the different narrative voices and the control of structure.

A verse from a spiritual serves as the epigram of "The Welcome Table" (which is dedicated "for sister Clara Ward") and at once provides the source of the story's title and a preview of the narrative action.

> I'm going to sit at the Welcome table
> Shout my troubles over
> Walk and talk with Jesus
> Tell God how you treat me
> One of these days! (p. 81)

The table suggests both the altar or communion table of a church and the table that God as shepherd prepares "in the presence of my enemies" (Ps. 23:5). The Word "Welcome" is genuine in the sense that God sets the table and, as a good hostess, welcomes us to the overflowing cup; it is ironic in the sense that the people in the church are not able to welcome everyone to their table.

In the first section, with its ironic narrative voice, Walker manages to add dimension to what might seem at first rather transparent social criticism. The narrator—an observer of the old woman's arrival at the church, the confrontations, her sitting in the pew, the men carrying her out, the continued worship—never lets us see anything from the point of view of the woman; even the narrator's descriptions of the woman mixes objectivity, speculation, and prejudice. The narrator does know the thoughts and feelings of some of the people at the church and seems to be mingling with the crowd: "Some ... spoke words about her that were hardly fit to be heard, ... and some felt vague stirrings of pity, small and persistent and hazy" (pp. 81–82). The reader has a feeling that the narrator is present with, is even a member of, the congregation because of what the narrator observes about the preacher ("Did he say, as they thought he did, kindly, 'Auntie, you know this is not your church?'") and about the usher ("Did he call her 'Grandma,' as later he seemed to recall he had?" [p. 83]). Yet the narrator's own attitude is evident in the description of the ladies' reactions ("Could their husbands expect them to sit in church with *that?*") and especially in the section's final biting sentences, after the woman has been removed:

> Inside the church it was warmer. They sang, they prayed. The protection and promise of God's impartial love grew more not less desirable as the sermon gathered fury and lashed itself out above their penitent heads. (p. 84)

The background of the incident, of course, lies in the kneel-ins of the 1960s, but Walker freshens and intensifies the account by picturing a kneel-in not by militant young blacks, whose motives could at least be questioned, but by a small, frail, black woman who seems intent on worship. The narrator notes her concentration on the stained glass window, her "passionately ignoring" the church members, her "sharp *bothered* voice" when the usher interrupts her thoughts to ask her to leave (p. 83). Just as her rags and decay contrast with the finery and health of the church members, so her single-minded devotion contrasts with their mixed motives and fears and justifications. The reader gathers all this through Walker's able use of narrative voice.

The second section transfers the reader immediately to the perspective of the old woman. The narrator is still observer, watching the woman, but now the narrator also sees what the woman sees and knows what she experiences. In the first paragraph, we learn that in the church "she had been singing in her head" and that now she "saw something ... coming" (p. 84). The change in narrative perspective makes her walk and conversation with Jesus credible. We are able to see and hear what she sees and hears, and her supernatural experience is reported to us in a perfectly natural way. On the one hand, we know her meeting with Jesus occurs only in her own perception of reality (in the third section, we are told that people saw her walking alone, "jabbering" and "singing" [p. 87]).

On the other hand, the meeting has about it an unmistakable realism. When we learn the reason for her sudden happiness, it is through this sentence: "For coming down the highway at a firm though leisurely pace was Jesus" (p. 85). The sentence which precedes that one almost seems to break the narrative voice briefly and provide a moment of objectivity: "It became apparent why she was so happy" (p. 85). That seems to come from someone standing apart from her (apparent to whom?) and is not consistent with the rest of the narrative voice in this section which, though it is in the third person ("she looked," "she told," "she felt"), still rests within her consciousness. Is this a slip by Walker or a device to gain objectivity for this subjective experience? Whatever the case, both that sentence and the easy, natural description of the encounter make the reader believe its reality.

The two sections differ not only in point of view but also in tone. The irony of the first section has been noted, and perhaps the brief quotation gave a feeling for a certain flatness in the style, a pattern of understatement, a distinct distance between the narrator and the people whose consciousness the narrator observed, even though the narrator almost seemed a part of that consciousness, seemed one of the people. Phrases such as "terror of the unknown" (p. 81), "riotous anarchists" (p. 82), "desecration of Holy Church" (p. 82), "cold and clammy" (p. 82), "bloodless gray arthritic hands" (p. 84), as well as the repeated reference to the cold weather and the haughty people, contribute to the serious-minded, ironic atmosphere of the first section. In the second section, the language immediately shifts: "She . . . saw something interesting and delightful coming. She started to grin, toothlessly, with short giggles of joy, jumping about and slapping her hands on her knees" (p. 84). Then the description of Jesus contrasts sharply with the dull, gray images of the first section: "He was wearing an immaculate white, long dress trimmed in gold around the neck and hem, and a red, a bright red, cape. Over his left arm he carried a brilliant blue blanket" (p. 85). Throughout the section there is reference to ecstasy and excitement, singing and smiling, and in the final paragraph we are told that she is no longer tired and that Jesus' smiles are "like first clean ripples across a stagnant pond" (p. 86). The section has a brightness about it that is appropriate to the revelation the woman experiences, underscoring the true welcome she now re-

ceives and contrasting with the rejection and the irony of the first
section.

The final part backs away from brightness and vision. The narrator
seems remote again, and the verbs suggest tentativeness: "seemed,"
"appeared," "wondered," "guessed" (p. 87). An old woman was
found dead, we are told, and neither the narrator nor the people seem
to know much about her. That the narrator knows the minds of both
black and white observers adds new perspective to this final section,
and neither group comes off especially well. The people of the church
"never mentioned her to one another or to anybody else," though
"most of them heard sometime later that an old colored woman fell
dead along the highway" (pp. 86–87). The black families saw her
"high-stepping down the highway" but "wondered" where she might
be going, "guessed maybe she had relatives across the river" and never
"really knew," though she lived only a half-mile from the church
along the same road from which she was watched. The observers in
this final section seem puzzled and indifferent to the old woman, but
the words Walker uses for their description of her suggest that perhaps
she had qualities they lacked: "high-stepping," "insistent voice,"
"singing," "gesturing excitedly," "silent and smiling, looking at the
sky," "going so stoutly" (p. 87). She seems strange to them, walking
"herself to death" and wearing "her heart out," but because we have,
in a sense, shared her vision, she may seem to us heroic, noble.

To a certain extent, this story offers social criticism aimed at the
resistance of the white church to an acceptance of black people either
as church members or as human beings. We have noted, however, that
Walker is not strident in that criticism, using the ironic narrator and
changing the narrative voice in order to tone down the attack. Even
the identity of this church as "white" is ambiguous (the only reference
is to a "big white church" [p. 82], a phrase that could describe either
the race of the members or the color of the paint). One could argue
that Walker does not need to be explicit, since the reaction to the black
woman makes certain the race of the church members, but the ambiguity is nonetheless significant. It tones down the attack on whites in
general. It raises the issue of the failure of the church, as institutionalized Christianity, to live up to its own proclamation of "God's
impartial love"; or it may suggest that institutionalized religion—not
just white people, not just Christians—magnifies pride and respectability and demeans itself by demeaning those who for whatever reason
do not fit into the social class of the religious group. This is not to deny
that Walker is leveling sharp criticism at the white church. She is, and

she is justified in doing so. Still, the story has a value broader than the kneel-ins of the 1960s and can lead us to examine our longings for exclusiveness in various areas of our lives.

Yet another irony of the story might puzzle and delight the reader. The Jesus whom the old woman meets is just like the picture of Jesus the old woman had taken from a white woman's Bible. The Jesus she meets is the Jesus of Western civilization: neat, brown-haired, with a beautiful smile. This is no black messiah. She sees the Jesus whose picture—albeit stolen—hangs over her bed; except that her Jesus on the road is "not carrying in his arms a baby sheep" (p. 85); he is the same Good Shepherd she expected him to be. This interesting twist both makes a connection with the spiritual in the epigram and its image of the table prepared by the Shepherd/God, and it leaves the black woman with the white woman's savior.

When the old black woman complains about the treatment whites have given her people, Jesus only looks "at her kindly but in silence" (p. 86). Has she been deceived by this Jesus? Is it possible that she has been done in by the whites even in this revelation? Or could it be that Walker has offered two contrasting visions of Christianity: one expressed in the fear and exclusiveness of the church, the other in the simple joy and pleasure of the old woman's vision? The story invites us to ask such questions and is certainly not unambiguous about the meaning of the woman's revelation. Had the story ended with her walking with Jesus, its meaning might have been clearer. By returning to the more detached narrator, and by leaving the reader with the word that none of the black families "really knew" whether this woman had relatives across the river, Walker challenges the bliss of that joyful walk and makes us wonder about the woman, about Jesus, about religious experience, and ultimately, about ourselves.

The focus on black women in Alice Walker's fiction combines with her talents as a writer to provide literature that goes beyond a single issue and raises universal questions. "The Welcome Table" is a case in point. Though on first reading it may seem to offer simple social criticism, the story really stands up well under examination and gives readers, despite its brevity, many engaging topics for discussion. We have concentrated here on its structure and narrative voice as a means of demonstrating how readers might approach a story from those particular elements of fiction; other approaches may also suggest themselves. The notes on the religious questions in the story may hint at other paths for exploration. We have only dealt indirectly with the role of community in the story, and we began the chapter talking about the importance of community for Walker's fiction. Curiously enough, one emphasis of this story might be that, for all their strengths, communities sometimes forget the outcast, sometimes ignore, or worse, isolate the person who is for some reason different—the old, the unclean, the black. The black writer's "sense of community" includes awareness of exclusion's pain.

10

REYNOLDS PRICE
"A CHAIN OF LOVE"

Reynolds Price is a contemporary Southern writer who has translated some biblical stories and has written about the value of narrative for human survival—whether a person is listening to or telling the tales.[1] He cites the earliest narratives we have, those from the Hebrew Scriptures—the stories of Genesis and Judges, for example—and links the hearing and telling of those narratives with the growth and nurture of a people. His point is that the stories we hear as we mature can be the instruments by which we sense our own worth and learn what is necessary for our lives. Precisely through the story, a reader can be caught up in mystery, rescued from danger, given the word that matters. Further, by attempting to recover the order of past events and by asking for explanations, human beings not only come to understand their world and lives but are carried beyond themselves to deeper realities.[2] For Price, then, as a writer of fiction, a strong story line is crucial. In making such a case, he does not stand in the avant-garde of modern fiction, where traditional narrative forms are sometimes devalued and where the nonsense and chaos of human experience are prominent. But he does work within a long tradition of storytelling that, indeed, goes back to biblical times and that has been renewed in many countries through many centuries, not least in the American South in this century.

Reynolds Price now lives near Durham, North Carolina, and is the James B. Duke Professor of English at Duke University. He was born in 1933 in Macon, North Carolina, not a hundred miles from Durham, and has lived most of his life in that same section of the state. He graduated from Duke and then studied for three years at Oxford University as a Rhodes Scholar. He has found it important to live in a part of the country where he was raised, close to family roots—they were people who loved words and told stories[3]—and to form for himself "a stationary life where I could know a place, know the people."[4] His first novel, A Long and Happy Life, appeared in 1962, and since then he has published four novels, two collections of short fiction, two plays, and numerous essays and poems.[5] His stories are not always easy to understand at first reading (good stories seldom are), but they are not obscure or nonsensical by any means. They belong to a strong American tradition of purposeful narrative, intended to communicate with the reader, intended, Price says, to be truthful, to be entertaining, and to illuminate human problems.[6]

<h1 style="text-align:center">I</h1>

"A Chain of Love" was one of Reynolds Price's earliest stories. It is the first story in The Names and Faces of Heroes[7] and is about the same Mustian family, from rural North Carolina, who were central characters in A Long and Happy Life. Both Price's comic spirit and his seriousness of purpose are evident in this story. Told from the point of view of Rosacoke Mustian, a girl of high-school age, the story records Rosacoke's grandfather's admission to a hospital in Raleigh, her stay with him through several nights and days, and her experience with the illness and death of a man across the hall. In one sense, nothing much *happens* in the story; the plot is certainly not involved, though a great deal is going on inside Rosacoke, and what goes on there is available to the reader and forms the major strength of the narrative. The characters of the story really come alive: Rosacoke, her grandfather (Papa), her Mama, and her two brothers, Rato and Milo, are believable partly because of what we know of their life circumstances and partly because of the language Price uses, both the descriptive language and the words he puts in their mouths. Along with the humor of the story, the reader also is confronted, as Rosacoke is, with the painful reality of death. The humor keeps the story from becoming melodramatic or sentimental and, in a way, forms the framework from which both author and characters examine life.

That the story might be about death is evident from the opening paragraphs. The first paragraph alone contains four allusions to death: the time of year identified as "the dead of winter," Rato almost freezing "to death" making hand-turned ice cream for Papa's birthday, Papa saying "he would die at home if it was his time," and mention of the death of Papa's wife (pp. 3–4). The references continue, sometimes serious, sometimes casual. The doctor tells the family they won't need "a full-time nurse with two strong grandchildren dying to sit" with Papa at the hospital. Rosacoke recalls the Saturday night date she will miss with her boyfriend Wesley, and she remembers that as they sit in his Pontiac in front of her house the "rain frogs would be singing-out . . . and then . . . calming as if they had all died together." There is a sentence about the death of Rosacoke's own father and the note that Rato "had seen a lot of things die" (pp. 4–5).

Despite all these references to death, the tone at the beginning of the story seems lighthearted, even comical. That comes about partly because of the language Price uses and partly because of the interesting details and implications: we are given information that is suggestive of another story somewhere beneath the surface, and we are told some things that may seem irrevelant to the present story but in their vividness and reality make the present story more believable. For example, look at the reason Mama cannot stay at the hospital with her father-in-law:

> It worried her not being able to stay when staying was her duty, but they were having a Children's Day at the church that coming Sunday—mainly because the Christmas pageant had fallen through when John Arthur Bobbitt passed around the German measles like a dish of cool figs at the first rehearsal—and since she had organized the Sunbeams single-handed, she couldn't leave them then right on the verge of public performance. (p. 4)

The details of that sentence contribute to both the humor and the realism of the story.

The narrative perspective is not really clear until the third paragraph, when we learn that Rosacoke "almost liked the idea" (p. 4) of staying with her grandfather. Her one problem, we learn, will be missing her Saturday night with Wesley and "telling him goodbye without a word" (p. 5). In a very short space and through an indirect method, the narrator reveals that Mama does not entirely approve of her dating Wesley; that "telling him goodbye" was the "best part of any week" and had a special, almost mystical quality about it; that she would be happy to miss school for a week; that she liked being with Papa; and that she could not really remember much about her own father, who had been "run over by a green pick-up truck one Saturday evening late a long time ago" (pp. 4–5). Thus, in the first paragraph, where we recognize the central consciousness of the narrative, we learn a great deal about her, and we get it almost incidentally. We are not directly told Rosacoke's feelings; rather, we seem to be listening in on her thoughts and catching implications. That Rosacoke is always spoken of in the third person contributes to this sense of indirection.

The heart of the story, however, has to do with Rosacoke's experience with death in a room near Papa's. Early in the week the room had been empty, and while Papa slept she had gone there to look out the window at a statue of Jesus on the hospital lawn. Though she couldn't see the face on the statue from this window, she had remembered from their arrival at the hospital that it was the "kindest face she had ever seen," and she had stood in the room to "recollect his face the way she knew it was" (pp. 10–11; this scene prefigures events in the final story of the collection, the title story, "The Names and Faces of Heroes"). Later, when a man with lung cancer is given the room, all the Mustians become interested in what is happening over there, as though somehow that man's health were related to Papa's health. Rosacoke especially follows the action across the hall, attracted in part by the dying man's son, who reminds her of Wesley, and drawn by both curiosity and sympathy to the death itself. When, on the next Sunday, Rosacoke takes the flowers she has asked Mama to bring and attempts to give them to the man's family, she walks in on a priest administering last rites. Rosacoke is at once embarrassed and struck with awe at the mystery of the candles, the annointing, the chanted Latin phrases, the black-robed priest, and the death before her. When Rosacoke returns to Papa's room and Rato comes in to tell them that the man has died, the focus turns to their own family and the face of death: Rosacoke watches Papa play solitaire a little more slowly, and she knows he is thinking.

> It wasn't as if he didn't know where he was going or what it would be like when he got there. He just trusted and he hoped for one thing, he tried to see to one last thing—for a minute he stopped his card playing and asked Mama could he die at home, and Mama told him he could. (p. 42)

The tone of the story becomes more serious by the final paragraphs, but Price still handles the scene on a low key, revealing a great deal about the characters, showing depth of emotion without manipulating the reader's feeling, and ending the story by a slight turning away from the somberness. The next-to-last paragraph ends with the passage quoted just above. The final paragraph draws us even further into Rosacoke's own reflections, as she tries to understand her feelings about the man's death. She knows there is something good about his death: "With all that beautiful dying song, hadn't he surely died sanctified?" (p. 42). But she has kept everything about it, including her visit to the man's room, to herself; she has said nothing to the man's son or to his family, and she has not even spoken her own sorrow at the death of this stranger. She finally says, there in Papa's room, that the death just didn't "seem right," that she felt as though she had gotten to know the man "real well" (pp. 42–43). The final sentence of the story describes, again indirectly, the depth of her feeling and the impact of the whole experience on her family:

> And her words hung in the room for a long time—longer than it took Papa to pick the cards up off the bed and lay them without a sound in the drawer, longer even than it would have taken Rosacoke to say goodbye to Wesley if it had been Saturday night and she had been at home. (p. 43)

This is a story about death. It is also a story about some real human beings as they face death, and without saying it all explicitly, Price manages to describe the "chain of love" that binds not only this family but all humanity.

Is this, in any sense, a Southern story? Perhaps it is mainly the language and the setting that make it Southern. Rosacoke's gesture of giving fresh flowers to the dying man is characteristic of people for whom hospitality and outward expressions of kindness seem natural and unaffected, but those are not traits only of Southerners, or for that matter of all Southerners. Several incidents raise a regional emphasis, but they do so only in a minor way and serve to reinforce the realism of the story. Mama brings candy to the hospital for Papa because, as she says, "nurses hung around a patient who had his own candy like Grant around Richmond" (p. 8). The dying man had only recently moved to Raleigh from Baltimore—which is clearly "north" to these Carolina folks—and his being a stranger contributes to Rosacoke's desire to visit and take flowers and makes her a little conscious of her own region: "She might be from Afton, N.C., but she knew better than to go butting into some man's sickroom, to a man on his deathbed, without an expression of her sympathy. And it had to be flowers" (p. 29). The relationship of the Mustians to Papa's black orderly may also mark a regional flavor of the story: there is some condescension as Papa speaks to "Snowball Mason" (as the man introduces himself), but there is also easy comradery between him and the Mustians; and when, on one occasion, Papa speaks harshly to the orderly, Rosacoke feels badly and is sensitive to Snowball's feelings: "He walked out of Papa's room with his ice-cream coat hanging off him as if somebody had unstarched it" (p. 16). The story is decidedly Southern in its language, characterization, and setting, all of which make it a realistic narrative. Nevertheless, it moves beyond regionalism to deal with universal circumstances and basic human emotions. Furthermore, the humor of the narrative keeps those universal elements from becoming ponderous and saves the story from sentimentality.

II

Although Price's stories are, for the most part, set in the South, principally in North Carolina and Virginia, he claims that he has never felt himself to be a "Southern novelist." He has said, "I am a novelist—who was reared and has lived most of his life in the South . . . my work is not, has never been *about* the South"; he does not feel that he has "chronicled the South" but that he has presented his "own world."[8] His comments raise a distinction important to our consideration of Southern writers and to the reading of modern literature in general. To "chronicle the South" would not necessarily mean to write historical novels like *Gone with the Wind* or even Gaines's *The Autobiography of Miss Jane Pittman*. A writer might also "chronicle the South" by including in a novel concern with the many experiences that have shaped life in the South: plantation life, slavery, agriculture, the Civil War, the Confederacy, the climate, racial conflict, the role of women, the image of the Southern gentleman, states' rights, segregation, civil rights, integration, the Bible, fundamentalist religious groups, mainline churches, and so on. Many Southern writers have attempted to describe what it means to live in their particular time and place in the light of all that preceded them and have found their interpretation illuminated by the complex of issues, institutions, and personalities that has brought them to their time and place. So Faulkner's twentieth-century characters will recall their nineteenth-century ancestors attempting to understand themselves, their family, their region; and Gaines will describe modern black people through the history of their enslavement and suffering.

The distinction Price makes is that his own characters are not absorbed with the history of the South or with trying to analyze their relationship to the South. Perhaps Alice Walker would say of him, also, that there is not a whiff of magnolia. His characters speak with a Southern accent, they live in rural areas or small Southern towns, and many of them never get outside eastern North Carolina. They are Southerners, but they are not obsessed with being Southerners. In a sense, they are new Southerners: Southerners raised in the South late enough not to remember grandfathers and great uncles who were Confederate veterans or grandmothers and great aunts who were Daughters of the Confederacy; Southerners raised late enough not to have attended one too many Confederate Memorial Day picnics or heard one too many Southern politician thumping his pulpit for states' rights and white supremacy. Some elements of the old South remain today, but fewer people are victims of its worst effects. Price's characters, even when they are essentially rural in their orientation, and even when they lived half a century ago, are still basically modern Southerners. Price explores his own world; his characters try to understand their world. Not that they have no concern for the past: they do, but it is a personal and family past, not the history of the entire culture, that most engages them.

Reynolds Price is, in other words, a different kind of Southern writer. He belongs to a new generation of storytellers who have the same background and climate with the others and who have inherited some of the same gifts—a love of place, a tradition of narrative, a sense of community, an ear for speech—but who apply those gifts a little differently. Other contemporary Southerners might well be considered a part of this generation, whatever their age. Among those who have lived in the South and write about the South but are no longer primarily concerned to fight the old South's battles, we might think of Doris Betts, Gail Godwin, James Dickey, Anne Tyler. If we ask whether the tradition of a strong Southern literature can continue once the variety of visions associated with the old South has faded, we have only to read these modern Southerners. A number of observers have felt that Southern literature prospered because of the Civil War and all that was associated with it. Perhaps a new generation of Southern writers will finally lead readers from all parts of the country beyond the old romances and tragedies to a sense of what it means to live anywhere in a decidedly modern world. The best Southern writers have lasted because, even when they wrote about Southern problems and issues, they managed to transcend their region and make clear the universal application of their fiction. It was not through their love for the American South that the Japanese and the French were among the first to applaud the work of Faulkner and O'Connor; it was because the writing was true, the characters and issues as compelling across the oceans as in Mississippi or Georgia.

Another dimension of Price's modernity is impressive, and that is his handling of religion. He has suggested that a major problem of the twentieth century is the "loss of faith."[9] That comes as no surprise to most people, of course; Flannery O'Connor said the same thing, and we could easily make a case for that loss having been experienced broadly in the nineteenth century as well (consider Matthew Arnold's poem "Dover Beach" and its conclusion that "the Sea of Faith was once, too, at the full. . . . But now I only hear/ Its melancholy, long, withdrawing roar"). Whereas Flannery O'Connor recognized the problem and sought through her fiction to correct it, Reynolds Price seems more inclined to describe the loss. He describes what life is like for people who suffer that loss and ways of managing to live in this modern age.

Price's characters express a variety of attitudes toward faith. A few of them, notably the rural Mustian family, are active churchgoers (the Mustians attend Delight Baptist Church); others seem never to think about church or to go to a church; others speak a brief prayer from time to time. The most secure of them, the ones most comfortable with their lives, seem to have found or developed some inner resources that sustain them, and they seem to act upon some human values centering primarily on attention to and love for other people, the giving and receiving of gifts. Some characters in his stories, Price says, are strong and secure enough to lead the searchers and strugglers to that safe harbor, that restful center for which all people yearn; they are the angels, he says, "tale-bearers of quite other orders of existence."[10] These characters (Price mentions Rena, Grainger, and Alice of *The Surface of the Earth*) seem to be modern people who are not known for piety or churchgoing, nor do they seem more perfect in their behavior than others, nor do they preach or admonish to faith. Rather, they live out their days, enjoy simple pleasures, and demonstrate their care of others.

His books do not demand, Price maintains, that the reader have any private information about the author's "personal convictions." I have been arguing that stories ought to stand on their own and be available to readers without secret knowledge, and Price's narratives do just that. (He himself feels readers may need "a Christian set of spectacles" to read Graham Greene or Flannery O'Connor; I have been saying that you don't need those spectacles to read O'Connor's stories but that perhaps a reader who is a Christian will put them on later for further reflection.)[11] Despite his avoidance of what he calls "doctrinal limitations" in his fiction, Price considers himself a Christian, "technically a Methodist," and feels that Christian values are important in his fiction. He says he has not been "an active member of the church" for "over twenty years" but the Christian faith is "maybe *the* central fact" of all his work: "That tragicomic vision of history as creation-fall-redemption-judgment-justice seems to me not only the most dramatic of all human conceptions but, quite simply, true to observable fact; above all to the facts of my own life."[12] The Christian values that are "visible" in his stories "tend to be what Aldous Huxley called the perennial philosophy, the basic values present in all great religions— values of charity and selflessness, which seem to me actually at the center of any possible durable ethic for human continuance on the globe."[13] We are not in the business of trying to evaluate the theological precision of Price's view of Christianity. We listen to him to get a sense of how this particular modern writer, who recognizes the loss of faith in our time, expresses his understanding of the values that are crucial to his work. He even says that he hopes his stories are "honestly and complicatedly proselytizing"[14]—the two qualifiers providing just the right tension.

Price writes about the modern South and about people who live firmly in the modern world. To the extent that Christian values are expressed in his fiction, they are not boldly symbolized but at once natural and hidden. Some of his people are perhaps the "anonymous Christians" theologian Karl Rahner talked about, and they may instruct others of us who live in a world that suffers the loss of faith.[15]

Comedy provides one of the links between Price's understanding of the South and his understanding of Christianity. He has said that "the great, enduring, saving trait of the American South has been its sense of humor, which has helped it through all its tragedies and follies."[16] The South may not have a better sense of humor than any other region, but Southern literature, to be sure, shows a rich vein of humor, and many families and communities seem to have endless funny tales to tell. Price recognizes the strength of this sense of humor and works it out in his own literature.

> All my work is comic—not by conscious choice but because in attempting to embody the world that I've known, I have portrayed a comic world. Comedy is almost always a function of experience, a function of life. Even in the intensest moments of despair, pain, grief, wild bursts of laughter will insist upon rising and asserting themselves.[17]

When asked whether his Christianity accounted for this "belief that existence is comic," Price responded:

> Very much so. I think insofar as I understand anything about comparative religion, that most of the great religions of the world would ultimately assert that reality is comic—if comic be taken to mean that ultimately all things tend toward order, serenity, the dissolution of the self in some larger intention which, in its broadest sense, would imply comic reality.... All things end, unavoidably, in happiness—divine will—though that will's schedule is generally a good deal slower than human beings like.[18]

Price's definition of the comic reminds us, of course, that comedy and humor are not exactly the same thing. When literary people talk about comedy, they are talking about a sense of order and happiness, not simply about funny stories. Even so, comedy and humor are related. The ability to laugh and see the humor in life's complexities is a way of understanding that, even when everything seems to be falling apart around us, the world still rolls on and that each new day is another gift of life (Price has called "morning" the "oldest gift").[19] Confidence that God is taking care of us and our world enables us both to see the ultimate order of all things and to laugh.[20]

Another point at which the Southernness and Christianity of Price's background come together is in the narrative itself. We have already noted his interest in biblical narrative. He has said that the stories of the Bible are "the most successful narratives in human history, in that they have enforced belief and attention upon thousands of years of auditors."[21] He has published his own translations of biblical narratives, including the complete Gospel of Mark, and he has recently written the foreword for a scholarly study of that Gospel.[22] Price also grew up with stories, not only the biblical stories that he read and heard as a young child but also the tales of his own family: on both his mother's and his father's sides of the family there were great storytellers always ready to tell and retell what had happened in their pasts.[23] Perhaps the tradition of his family contributed to it, as did his early familiarity with the Bible, but Price has also come to feel, as have many others, that human beings have a voracious "appetite for stories."[24] He says we long for narrative in our lives and especially for a narrative with the ring of truth about it, the narrative that seems to make sense of things and tell us more than we could guess from the ordinary details of our lives. Such a story might well be linked, according to Price, with divine reality; that is, our own longing for narrative is related to the way we understand ourselves and our world and takes us beyond ourselves toward new perspectives.[25] Thus, the Southernness and Christianity of Price's background come together in narrative and underscore the lasting significance of story.

Many modern writers reach toward this possibility for narrative. A story can be an appropriate response to the difficulties of modern life and our apparent loss of faith. Price feels "long watching, slow and incremental description" are needed in order to demonstrate how we might hold on and live in these days. "The long-breathed narrative forms—epic and novel—still seem to me the only literary forms capable of doing any sort of justice to the complexities of twentieth century life."[26] There again, the contemporary writer's vision merges with the biblical tradition, for it is precisely in the long and slow story of the people of Israel, and in the enduring narratives about Jesus and his first followers, and in the more hidden tale of the church growing, witnessing, serving, and worshipping down through the centuries that we see God's care of these people expressed and affirmed over and over. These narratives report the faith and encourage us to face our complexities. An interpreting community uses its imagination to read the stories of its own time and to understand these lasting tales of God's faithfulness.

NOTES

CHAPTER 1

1. Recent valuable studies include Giles B. Gunn, *The Interpretation of Otherness: Literature, Religion, and the American Imagination* (New York and London: Oxford University Press, 1979); Wesley A. Kort, *Moral Fiber: Character and Belief in Recent American Fiction* (Philadelphia: Fortress Press, 1982); William Mallard, *The Reflection of Theology in Literature: A Case Study in Theology and Culture* (San Antonio: Trinity University Press, 1977); Lynn Ross-Bryant, *Imagination and the Life of the Spirit* (Chico, Calif.: Scholars Press, 1981); and Amos Niven Wilder, *Theopoetic: Theology and the Religious Imagination* (Philadelphia: Fortress Press, 1976).

Important essays have been collected in several anthologies, including early volumes edited by Stanley Romaine Hopper, *Spiritual Problems in Contemporary Literature* (New York: Harper & Brothers, 1952), and by Nathan A. Scott, Jr., *The New Orpheus: Essays Toward a Christian Poetic* (New York and London: Sheed & Ward, 1964). More recent collections have been edited by Giles B. Gunn, *Literature and Religion* (New York: Harper & Row, 1971); Robert Detweiler, *Art/Literature/Religion: Life on the Borders*, JAAR Thematic Studies 49, no. 2 (1983); John R. Mulder, *Literature and Religion: The Convergence of Approaches*, *JAAR* 47, Supplement (June 1979); and G. B. Tennyson and Edward E. Ericson, Jr., *Religion and Modern Literature: Essays in Theory and Criticism* (Grand Rapids: Wm. B. Eerdmans, 1975).

In 1975 Norman Reed Cary and Vernon Ruland each published works that reviewed and evaluated major studies of literature and theology. See Cary, *Christian Criticism in the Twentieth Century: Theological Approaches to Literature* (Port Washington, N.Y.: Kennikat Press, 1975) and Ruland, *Horizons of Criticism: An Assessment of Religious-Literary Options* (Chicago: American Library Association, 1975).

Nathan A. Scott, Jr., who for many years directed the literature and theology program at the University of Chicago and now teaches at the University of Virginia, has written many books discussing the relationship of the two disciplines and analyzing literature. His contributions to the field include *The Broken Center: Studies in the Theological Horizon of Modern Literature* (New Haven, Conn.: Yale University Press, 1966); *The Poetry of Civic Virtue: Eliot, Malraux, Auden* (Philadelphia: Fortress Press, 1976); and *Negative Capability: Studies in the New Literature and the Religious Situation* (New Haven, Conn.: Yale University Press, 1969).

William F. Lynch has been one of the most prominent Roman Catholic interpreters: see his *Christ and Apollo: The Dimensions of the Literary Imagination* (Notre Dame, Ind.: University of Notre Dame Press, 1960) and *Christ and Prometheus: A New Image of the Secular* (Notre Dame, Ind.: University of Notre Dame Press, 1970).

Other helpful studies are John Coulson, *Religion and Imagination: "in aid of a grammar of assent"* (Oxford: Clarendon Press, 1981); Helen Gardner, *Religion and Literature* (New York and London: Oxford University Press, 1971); Frederick J. Hoffman, *The Imagination's New Beginning: Theology and Modern Literature* (Notre Dame, Ind.: University of Notre Dame Press, 1967); Wesley A. Kort, *Narrative Elements and Religious Meaning* (Philadelphia: Fortress Press, 1975); Paul A. Lacey, *The Inner War: Forms and Themes in Recent American Poetry* (Philadelphia: Fortress Press, 1972); Sallie TeSelle, *Literature and the Christian Life* (New Haven, Conn.: Yale University Press, 1966); Gerardus Van der Leeuw, *Sacred and Profane Beauty: The Holy in Art* (Nashville: Abingdon Press, 1963); Nelvin Vos, *The Drama of Comedy: Victim and Victor* (Richmond: John Knox Press, 1966); and Amos Niven Wilder (who, like Scott, has written extensively on this topic), *Theology and Modern Literature* (Cambridge: Harvard University Press, 1958).

One of the more important volumes from a conservative Christian position is Leland Ryken's *Triumphs of the Imagination: Literature in Christian Perspective* (Downers Grove, Ill.: Inter-Varsity Press, 1979).

Numerous separate articles have appeared, and many of the most valuable ones are included in the anthologies noted above. I mention here just two others for their methodological emphasis: Carol P. Christ, "Feminist Studies in Religion and Literature: A Methodological Reflection," *JAAR* 44 (June 1976): 317–25; and John W. Dixon, Jr., "Art as the Making of the World: Outline of Method in the Criticism of Religion and Art," *JAAR* 51 (March 1983): 15–36.

For a useful anthology of contemporary stories with an excellent introduction and afterword, see Robert Detweiler and Glenn Meeter, eds., *Faith and Fiction: The Modern Short Story* (Grand Rapids: Wm. B. Eerdmans, 1979).

2. A number of scholars make a case for pluralistic approaches; cf. Gunn, *Literature and Religion*, 21; Ruland, *Horizons of Criticism*, 58–59; David Tracy, *The Analogical Imagination: Christian Theology and the Culture of Pluralism* (New York: Crossroad, 1981).

3. While I could not begin to list all the books which have helped to shape my own theology, I would like to account for some influences. Former teachers, such as H. George Anderson, Martin J. Heinecken, William H. Lazareth, and Edmund A. Steimle, in their classroom work and in their own writing, have been extremely important. I am indebted to numerous other teachers and to a variety of theologians; the list could be quite long, and certain qualifications could be given with each name. Here it seems enough to note the theologians whose works have been the most significant for me, though the degree and reason for the influence varies greatly with each one: Dietrich Bonhoeffer, Robert Farrar Capon, Gustavo Gutiérrez, Sallie McFague, Jürgen Moltmann, Rosemary Radford Reuther, Joseph Sittler, and Paul Tillich.

4. On metaphor, see especially Sallie McFague's recent *Metaphorical Theology: Models of God in Religious Language* (Philadelphia: Fortress Press, 1982), as well as her earlier *Speaking in Parables: A Study in Metaphor and Theology* (Philadelphia: Fortress Press, 1975). Other helpful resources include Sheldon Sacks, ed., *On Metaphor* (Chicago: University of Chicago Press, 1979), and two volumes by Philip Wheelwright: *The Burning Fountain: A Study in the Language of Symbolism*, rev. ed. (Bloomington: Indiana Univer-

sity Press, 1968) and *Metaphor and Reality* (Bloomington: Indiana University Press, 1962).

5. Fyodor Dostoyevsky, *The Brothers Karamazov*, trans. Constance Garnett (New York: New American Library, 1957), 106, quoted in Jacques Maritain, *Creative Intuition in Art and Poetry* (New York: Meridian Books, 1953), 314.

6. Cf. Wilder, *Theopoetic*, 26, 46, 55; and Walter Stein, *Criticism as Dialogue* (Cambridge: Cambridge University Press, 1969), 70–71.

7. Flannery O'Connor, *The Complete Stories* (New York: Farrar, Straus & Giroux, 1981). See chapter 7 for discussion of her work.

8. Alice Walker, *In Love & Trouble: Stories of Black Women* (New York: Harcourt Brace Jovanovich, 1973). For discussion of Walker, see chapter 9.

9. Doris Betts, *Heading West* (New York: Alfred A. Knopf, 1981).

10. "The Boys of Winter," *Time* (7 February 1983): 66, 69.

11. On the "secret grace of God" working in human experience, see Karl Rahner, "Poetry and the Christian," in his *Theological Investigations* 4, trans. Kevin Smyth (Baltimore: Helicon Press, 1966), 357–67. On the natural as the "occasion" of grace, see Joseph Sittler, *Essays on Nature and Grace* (Philadelphia: Fortress Press, 1972), 86–87.

12. An orientation such as the one I present here has been discussed, criticized, and revamped many times in the church. The general position from which my own reflections come is formulated in the Lutheran Church in America's Social Statement on Church and State: A Lutheran Perspective, adopted by the Third Biennial Convention, Kansas City, Missouri, 21–29 June, 1966. Professor William H. Lazareth, who was influential in the development of that statement, has articulated and expanded such an approach in a number of places. Some years ago, he did so in his *A Theology of Politics* (New York: Board of Social Missions of the United Lutheran Church in America, 1960) and in his *Luther on the Christian Home* (Philadelphia: Muhlenberg Press, 1960). For more recent treatments, see his essays in William H. Lazareth, ed., *The Left Hand of God: Essays on Discipleship and Patriotism* (Philadelphia: Fortress Press, 1976) and in George W. Forell and William H. Lazareth, eds., *God's Call to Public Responsibility* (Philadelphia: Fortress Press, 1978). For other analyses of this and related issues, cf. Heinrich Bornkamm, *Luther's Doctrine of the Two Kingdoms in the Context of His Theology*, trans. Karl H. Hertz (Philadelphia: Fortress Press, 1966); Karl H. Hertz, ed., *Two Kingdoms and One World: A Sourcebook in Christian Social Ethics* (Minneapolis: Augsburg Publishing House, 1976) and Gustaf Wingren, *Creation and Law*, trans. Ross Mackenzie (Philadelphia: Muhlenberg Press, 1961).

13. For one of the places where Luther expresses this theme, see his letter to Philip Melanchthon, 1 August 1521, Letter 91, *Luther's Works*, Vol. 48, ed. and trans. Gottfried G. Krodel (Philadelphia: Fortress Press, 1963), 282.

14. Martin Luther, "Temporal Authority: To What Extent It Should Be Obeyed," trans. J. J. Schindel, *Luther's Works*, Vol. 45, rev. and ed. Walther I. Brandt (Philadelphia: Muhlenberg Press, 1962), 96.

CHAPTER 2

1. On the imagination, see especially the following: Jacob Bronowski, *The Origins of Knowledge and Imagination* (New Haven, Conn.: Yale University Press, 1978); Coulson, *Religion and Imagination*; Ray L. Hart, *Unfinished Man and the Imagination: Toward an Ontology and a Rhetoric of Revelation* (New York: Herder & Herder, 1968); Lynch, *Christ and Apollo*; Mark C. Taylor, ed., *Unfinished . . . : Essays in Honor of Ray L. Hart*, JAAR Thematic

Issue 48 (1981); Mary Warnock, *Imagination* (Berkeley: University of California Press, 1976); Amos Niven Wilder, *Jesus' Parables and the War of Myths: Essays on Imagination in the Scripture*, ed. James Breech (Philadelphia: Fortress Press, 1982); and Charles E. Winquist, ed., *The Archaeology of the Imagination*, JAAR Thematic Issue 48, no. 2 (1981).

2. Gail Godwin, *A Mother and Two Daughters* (New York: Viking Press, 1982).

3. George Bernard Shaw, *Saint Joan: A Chronicle Play in Six Scenes and an Epilogue* (Baltimore: Penguin Books, 1951), 59.

4. Cf. Lynch, *Christ and Apollo*, 23, and Coulson, *Religion and Imagination*, 6–8, 52.

5. Cf. Coulson, *Religion and Imagination*, 54.

6. For a forceful argument in behalf of a Christian literary criticism, see Ryken, *Triumphs of the Imagination*, 121–28.

CHAPTER 3

1. The literature is extensive, but the following books have been most helpful to me: Erich Auerbach, *Mimesis: The Representation of Reality in Western Literature* (Princeton, N.J.: Princeton University Press, 1953); Wayne C. Booth, *The Rhetoric of Fiction* (Chicago: University of Chicago Press, 1961); Stanley Fish, *Is There a Text in This Class? The Authority of Interpretive Communities* (Cambridge: Harvard University Press, 1980); Northrop Frye, *Anatomy of Criticism: Four Essays* (Princeton, 1957; reprint, New York: Atheneum, 1970); E. D. Hirsch, Jr., *The Aims of Interpretation* (Chicago: University of Chicago Press, 1976) and *Validity in Interpretation* (New Haven, Conn.: Yale University Press, 1967); C. S. Lewis, *An Experiment in Criticism* (Cambridge: Cambridge University Press, 1961); I. A. Richards, *Principles of Literary Criticism* (New York: Harcourt, Brace & Co., 1925); Robert Scholes and Robert Kellogg, *The Nature of Narrative* (New York and London: Oxford University Press, 1966); and Rene Wellek and Austin Warren, *Theory of Literature*, 3d ed. (New York: Harcourt, Brace & Co., 1956).

2. The works of Wesley A. Kort provide a good example of analysis of literature through elements of fiction: see his *Narrative Elements* and *Moral Fiber*.

3. John Gardner, *The Resurrection* (1966; New York: Ballantine Books, 1974).

4. Saul Bellow, *Herzog* (New York: Viking Press, 1964).

5. J. D. Salinger, *Franny and Zooey* (Boston: Little, Brown and Co., 1961).

6. Scholes and Kellogg, *Nature of Narrative*, 212.

7. William Faulkner, *Absalom, Absalom!* (1936; reprint, New York: Vintage Books, 1972).

8. Walker, *In Love & Trouble*, 81; I will discuss this story further in chapter 9.

9. Kort, *Narrative Elements*, 9.

10. Paul Ricoeur, "The Symbol Gives Rise to Thought," in Gunn, *Literature and Religion*, 211.

11. Cf. Wheelwright, *The Burning Fountain*, 9–11, and *Metaphor and Reality*, 92–110; Wellek and Warren, *Theory of Literature*, 189.

12. Frye, *Anatomy of Criticism*, 99.

13. Cf. also Maud Bodkin, *Archetypal Patterns in Poetry: Psychological Studies of Imagination* (London: Oxford University Press, 1934).

14. Kort, *Narrative Elements*, 20, 39.

15. Susan Sontag, *Against Interpretation and Other Essays* (New York: Farrar, Straus & Giroux, 1966), 32.

16. Cf. Fish, *Is There a Text in This Class?* 32, 67, 86, 318, 371; Hirsch, *Aims*, 79–80; Scholes and Kellogg, *Nature of Narrative,* 82–105.

17. Flannery O'Connor, *Mystery and Manners: Occasional Prose*, ed. Sally and Robert Fitzgerald (New York: Noonday Press, 1961), 73.

18. Ibid., 96.

19. Ibid.

20. William Faulkner, *Intruder in the Dust* (1948; reprint, New York: Vintage Books, 1972).

21. Madison Jones, *A Cry of Absence* (New York: Pocket Books, 1972).

22. The humorous stories of the old Southern frontier—Virginia and the Carolinas westward to Arkansas and Louisiana—have been a rich resource for later generations of American writers, especially those who spring from the same region. These tall tales begin, in part, with accounts of Davy Crockett's adventures and are continued throughout the nineteenth century by writers such as Augustus Baldwin Longstreet, William Tappan Thompson, George Washington Harris, and Mark Twain. Selections from this literature appear in *Humor of the Old Southwest*, ed. Hennig Cohen and William B. Dillingham (Boston: Houghton Mifflin, 1964).

23. William Faulkner, *The Hamlet* (New York: Random House, 1940); *The Town* (New York: Random House, 1957); *The Mansion* (New York: Random House, 1959).

24. Frye, *Anatomy of Criticism*, 86–87. Cf. also Fish, *Is There a Text in This Class?* 161–63; Hirsch, *Aims*, 8, 90; Wellek and Warren, *Theory of Literature*, 42, 148; Monroe C. Beardsley and W. K. Wimsatt, "The Intentional Fallacy," in Wimsatt's *The Verbal Icon: Studies in the Meaning of Poetry* (Lexington, Ky.: University of Kentucky, 1954), 3–18.

25. For discussion of the reader's role, see Fish, *Is There a Text in This Class?* 48, 158–65, 379–80; Kort, *Narrative Elements*, 12–13; and Lewis, *Experiment in Criticism*, 36–37, 85, 107, 130. Much recent criticism has given new—and, in some cases, extensive—significance to the reader through what is called "reader-response theory." For academic treatment of this development and for additional bibliography, see, for example, Stephen Mailloux, *Interpretive Conventions: The Reader in the Study of American Fiction* (Ithaca, N.Y.: Cornell University Press, 1982); Jane P. Tompkins, ed., *Reader-Response Criticism: From Formalism to Post-Structuralism* (Baltimore: Johns Hopkins University Press, 1980); and W. Daniel Wilson, "Readers in Texts," *PMLA* 96 (October 1981): 848–63. Tompkins's book contains an annotated bibliography, 233–72.

CHAPTER 4

1. Hirsch, *Aims*, 122–23.

2. Walker Percy, *The Second Coming* (New York: Farrar, Straus & Giroux, 1980).

3. Samuel Taylor Coleridge, *Biographia Literaria* 2 (1817; reprint, Berkeley, Calif.: The Scholar Press, 1971), 2.

4. Anne Tyler, *Dinner at the Homesick Restaurant* (New York: Alfred A. Knopf, 1982).

5. Cf. D. S. Savage, "Truth and the Art of the Novel," in Scott, *New Orpheus*, 290–304, for another perspective on this issue.

6. Faulkner, *The Town*, 296; cf. also Warren Beck, *Man in Motion: Faulkner's Trilogy* (Madison: University of Wisconsin Press, 1961).

7. Wellek and Warren, *Theory of Literature*, 243.

8. William Faulkner, *As I Lay Dying* (1930; reprint, New York: Vintage Books, 1964).

9. O'Connor, *Mystery and Manners*, 45.
10. John Killinger, *The Fragile Presence: Transcendence in Modern Literature* (Philadelphia: Fortress Press, 1973), 4, 9. See also his *The Failure of Theology in Modern Literature* (Nashville: Abingdon Press, 1963).
11. For one of Faulkner's accounts of the writing and rewriting of *Sanctuary* (1931; reprint, New York: Random House, 1962), see Frederick L. Gwynn and Joseph L. Blotner, eds., *Faulkner in the University: Class Conferences at the University of Virginia, 1957–1958* (New York: Vintage Books, 1965), 90–91.
12. For a very different viewpoint, see Peter Thorpe, *Why Literature Is Bad for You* (Chicago: Nelson-Hall, 1980) and Duncan Williams, *Trousered Apes* (New Rochelle, N.Y.: Arlington House, 1972).
13. Cf. Faulkner's Nobel Prize acceptance speech for one of his statements about these virtues; see James B. Meriwether, ed., *Essays, Speeches & Public Letters by William Faulkner* (New York: Random House, 1965), 118–21.
14. O'Connor, *Mystery and Manners*, 107–18.
15. In her early and important study *Literature and the Christian Life*, Sallie [McFague] TeSelle criticized scholars like Nathan A. Scott, Jr., for dwelling on the negative and ignoring the joyful elements of contemporary literature; see 49.
16. Elder Olson, *On Value Judgments in the Arts and Other Essays* (Chicago: University of Chicago Press, 1976), 326. Cf. also Hirsch, *Aims*, 122–23.

CHAPTER 5

1. Fish, *Is There a Text in This Class?*
2. Tracy, *The Analogical Imagination*, 116, 120.
3. Stanley Hauerwas, *A Community of Character: Toward a Constructive Christian Ethic* (Notre Dame, Ind.: University of Notre Dame Press, 1981), 52, 65, 92. Cf. also reviews of various positions relating community and narrative in Michael Goldberg, *Theology and Narrative: A Critical Introduction* (Nashville: Abingdon Press, 1981) and Clarence P. Walhout, "Literary Criticism in the Christian Community," *Christian Scholars Review* 8 (1979): 295–306.
4. Sittler, *Essays on Nature and Grace*, 118–19.
5. Amos Niven Wilder, *Early Christian Rhetoric: The Language of the Gospel* (London: SCM Press, 1964), 126, 128.
6. Luther, "Temporal Authority," 91–92.
7. Numerous recent studies discuss the importance of narrative in the Bible. Cf. especially Robert Alter, *The Art of Biblical Narrative* (New York: Basic Books, 1981); James Barr, "Story and History in Biblical Theology," *Journal of Religion* 56 (January 1976): 1–17; Robert McAfee Brown, "My Story and 'The Story,'" *Theology Today* 32 (July 1975): 166–73; Brevard Childs, *The Book of Exodus: A Critical, Theological Commentary* (Philadelphia: Westminster Press, 1974); Hans W. Frei, *The Eclipse of Biblical Narrative: A Study in Eighteenth- and Nineteenth-Century Hermeneutics* (New Haven, Conn.: Yale University Press, 1974); Wilder, *Early Christian Rhetoric*; and John E. Zuck, "Tales of Wonder: Biblical Narrative, Myth, and Fairy Stories," *JAAR* 44 (1976): 299–308. On Wilder's work, see John Dominic Crossan, *A Fragile Craft: The Work of Amos Niven Wilder* (Chico, Calif.: Scholars Press, 1981).
8. Again, there is extensive literature on this subject. In addition to the works already cited in this chapter (especially Alter, Goldberg, Hauerwas, Tracy, and Wilder) and works noted in earlier chapters (Auerbach; Coulson, 151; Kort; and Scholes and Kellogg), see the following studies: John Navonne, *The Jesus Story: Our Life as Story in Christ* (Collegeville, Minn.: Liturgical

Press, 1979); Robert P. Roth, *Story and Reality: An Essay on Truth* (Grand Rapids: Wm. B. Eerdmans, 1973); George W. Stroup, *The Promise of Narrative Theology: Recovering the Gospel in the Church* (Atlanta: John Knox Press, 1981); Brian Wicker, *The Story-Shaped World: Fiction and Metaphysics; Some Variations on a Theme* (Notre Dame, Ind.: University of Notre Dame Press, 1975); James B. Wiggins, ed., *Religion as Story* (New York: Harper & Row, 1975); Amos Niven Wilder, *The New Voice: Religion, Literature, Hermeneutics* (New York: Herder & Herder, 1969); Charles E. Winquist, *Homecoming: Interpretation, Transformation, and Individuation* (Missoula, Mont.: Scholars Press, 1978). Among many valuable articles are Stephen Crites, "The Narrative Quality of Experience," *JAAR* 39 (September 1971): 291–311; Julián Marías, "Philosophic Truth and the Metaphoric System," in *Interpretation: The Poetry of Meaning*, ed. Stanley Romaine Hopper and David L. Miller (New York: Harcourt, Brace & Co., 1967), 41–53. Johann Baptist Metz, "A Short Apology of Narrative," *Concilium* n.s. 5 (1973). 84–96; and Harold Weinrich, "Narrative Theology," *Concilium* n.s. 5 (1973): 46–56. The October 1983 issue of *Interpretation* (37:339–401) is devoted to "Narrative and Theology" and includes essays by Gabriel Fackre, Amos Niven Wilder, S. W. Sykes, and Stanley Hauerwas, as well as expository articles (of biblical texts) by John Dominic Crossan, Michael Goldberg, and Walter Wink. Some writers today feel that modern experience is no longer orderly, and so they attempt to write an objective, nonnarrative fiction; for discussion of postmodern fiction and its approach to narrative, see Scott, *Negative Capability*, 25–58.

9. Reynolds Price, *A Palpable God: Thirty Stories Translated from the Bible with an Essay on the Origins and Life of Narrative* (New York: Atheneum, 1978), 27; cf. also 17, 19, 45.

10. See ibid., and Elie Wiesel, *Messengers of God: Biblical Portraits and Legends* (New York: Random House, 1976). Clarence Jordan retold many portions of the New Testament: see, for example, his *The Cotton Patch Version of Luke and Acts: Jesus' Doings and Happenings* (New York: Association Press, 1969) and *The Cotton Patch Version of Paul's Epistles* (New York: Association Press, 1968).

11. John Gardner, *On Moral Fiction* (New York: Basic Books, 1978), 29.

12. Cf. Richard A. Jensen, *Telling the Story: Variety and Imagination in Preaching* (Minneapolis: Augsburg Publishing House, 1980); Eugene Lowry, *The Homiletical Plot: The Sermon as Narrative Art Form* (Atlanta: John Knox Press, 1980); McFague, *Speaking in Parables*; Charles L. Rice, *Interpretation and Imagination: The Preacher and Contemporary Literature* (Philadelphia: Fortress Press, 1970); Edmund A. Steimle, Morris J. Niedenthal, and Charles L. Rice, *Preaching the Story* (Philadelphia: Fortress Press, 1975).

13. See especially Lowry, *The Homiletical Plot*.

14. Though scholars have known about the manuscript of "Father Abraham" for years, it was not published until 1983, in a very limited edition; it should be available soon in a trade edition. Professor James B. Meriwether, the prominent Faulkner scholar who edited the story, has said, "The young Faulkner did nothing more ambitious or more successful." *Time* (13 June 1983): 67.

15. Hart, *Unfinished Man and the Imagination*, 60–62; Hirsch, *Aims*, 4–5.

PART II

1. In this area also, there are vast resources. Three important reference works should assist readers in learning about Southern literature: Robert Bain, Joseph M. Flora, and Louis D. Rubin, Jr., eds. *Southern Writers: A*

Bibliographical Dictionary (Baton Rouge and London: Louisiana State University Press, 1979); Louis D. Rubin, Jr., ed., *A Bibliographical Guide to the Study of Southern Literature* (Baton Rouge and London: Louisiana State University Press, 1969); and Jay B. Hubbell, *The South in American Literature: 1607–1900* (Durham, N.C.: Duke University Press, 1954). In addition to the resources identified in these reference works, readers may also wish to consult a recent, valuable collection of essays: Philip Castille and William Osborne, eds., *Southern Literature in Transition: Heritage and Promise* (Memphis: Memphis State University Press, 1983).

2. Nathan A. Scott, Jr., in Detweiler, *Arts/Literature/Religion*, 142–45; cf. also Scott's *Negative Capability*, 3–58, and his *Broken Center*, 1–24, for further discussion of new fiction.

3. Robert Penn Warren, *All the King's Men* (New York: Harcourt, Brace & Co., 1946).

4. Faulkner, *Absalom, Absalom!*

5. See Cleanth Brooks's discussion of the role of the community in Faulkner's *Light in August* entitled "The Community and the Pariah," in *William Faulkner: The Yoknapatawpha Country* (New Haven, Conn.: Yale University Press, 1963), 52–55.

6. O'Connor, *Mystery and Manners*, 44–45. For a related analysis—though one not concerned primarily with literature—see James McBride Dabbs, *Haunted by God: The Cultural and Religious Experience of the South* (Richmond: John Knox Press, 1972).

CHAPTER 6

1. Gwynn and Blotner, *Faulkner in the University*, 86.

2. Ibid., 117.

3. James B. Meriwether and Michael Millgate, eds., *Lion in the Garden: Interviews with William Faulkner, 1926–1962* (New York: Random House, 1968), 253.

4. Ibid., 100.

5. William Faulkner, *Light in August* (New York: Smith and Haas, 1932), 210–13. Recent paperback editions by Modern Library and Vintage Books have been reproduced photographically from a copy of the first printing and so have the same pagination.

6. Francis L. Kunkel, "Christ Symbolism in Faulkner: Prevalence of the Human," *Renascence* 17 (Spring 1965): 148–56; Virginia V. Hlavsa, "St. John and Frazer in *Light in August*: Biblical Form and Mythic Function," *Bulletin of Research in the Humanities* 83 (Spring 1980): 9–26.

7. Faulkner, *Light in August*, 98.

8. Meriwether and Millgate, *Lion in the Garden*, 178.

9. Ibid., 178–79.

10. William Faulkner, *A Fable* (New York: Random House, 1954). For discussion of Faulkner's use of Christian images in this novel, see my essay, "The Christ Story in *A Fable*," *Mississippi Quarterly* 23 (Summer 1970): 251–64, and more recently, Rosemary M. Magee, "*A Fable* and the Gospels: A Study in Contrasts," *Research Studies* (Washington State University) 47 (June 1979): 98–107.

11. William Faulkner, *Collected Stories* (New York: Random House, 1950), 225–27. The story was first published in the *American Mercury* 36 (October 1935): 156–68.

12. Cf. Noel E. Polk, "Faulkner and Respectability," in *Fifty Years of Yoknapatawpha: Faulkner and Yoknapatawpha, 1979*, ed. Doreen Fowler and Ann J. Abadie (Jackson: University Press of Mississippi, 1980), 110–33;

Joseph W. Reed, Jr., *Faulkner's Narrative* (New Haven, Conn.: Yale University Press, 1973), 39–41; and Edmund L. Volpe, "Faulkner's 'Uncle Willy': A Childhood Fable," *Mosaic* 12 (1978): 177–81.
13. Faulkner, *Collected Stories*, 225.
14. Ibid., 231.
15. Cf. Polk, "Faulkner and Respectability," 118.
16. Gwynn and Blotner, *Faulkner in the University*, 36.
17. Faulkner, *Collected Stories*, 244.
18. Meriwether and Millgate, *Lion in the Garden*, 100.

CHAPTER 7

1. O'Connor, *Mystery and Manners*, 155.
2. Ibid., 146.
3. Ibid., 118.
4. Flannery O'Connor, *The Habit of Being*, ed. Sally Fitzgerald (New York: Farrar, Straus & Giroux, 1979), 100.
5. Ibid., 92.
6. O'Connor, *Mystery and Manners*, 192.
7. Ibid., 114.
8. O'Connor, *The Habit of Being*, 290.
9. O'Connor, *Mystery and Manners*, 162.
10. O'Connor, *The Habit of Being*, 424.
11. Ibid., 427.
12. Ibid., 592–94.
13. O'Connor, *The Complete Stories*, 519. All further references to this work appear in the text.
14. Cf. William V. Davis, " 'Large and Startling Figures': The Place of 'Parker's Back' in Flannery O'Connor's Canon," *Antigone Review* 28 (Winter 1977): 71–87. So much has been written about Flannery O'Connor and about this story in particular that I cannot begin to list all the criticism. I refer the interested reader to the thorough bibliography by Robert E. Golden in Robert E. Golden and Mary C. Sullivan, *Flannery O'Connor and Caroline Gordon: A Reference Guide* (Boston: G. K. Hall, 1977). The most important individual studies of "Parker's Back" are the following: Frederick Asals, *Flannery O'Connor: The Imagination of Extremity* (Athens, Ga.: University of Georgia Press, 1982), 126–27; André Bleikasten, "Writing on the Flesh: Tattoos and Taboos in 'Parker's Back,' " *Southern Literary Journal* 14 (Spring 1982): 8–18; Leon Driskell, " 'Parker's Back' vs. 'The Partridge Festival': Flannery O'Connor's Critical Choice," *Georgia Review* 21 (Winter 1967): 476–90; Caroline Gordon, "Heresy in Dixie," *Sewanee Review* 76 (Spring 1968): 263–97; Marion Montgomery, "Flannery O'Connor's Transformation of the Sentimental, *Mississippi Quarterly* 25 (1971): 1–18; Dennis Patrick Slattery, "Faith in Search of an Image: The Iconic Dimension of Flannery O'Connor's 'Parker's Back,' " *South Central Bulletin* 41 (Winter 1981): 120–23. For critics who have expressed special difficulty with Flannery O'Connor's orientation, see Carol Shloss, *Flannery O'Connor's Dark Comedies: The Limits of Inference* (Baton Rouge: Louisiana State University Press, 1980) and André Bleikasten, "The Heresy of Flannery O'Connor," in *Les Américanistes: New French Criticism on Modern American Fiction*, ed. Ira D. Johnson and Christiane Johnson (Port Washington, N.Y.: Kennikat Press, 1978).
15. Material from the manuscripts is quoted with the permission of Flannery O'Connor's literary executor, Robert Fitzgerald. The drafts of "Parker's Back" are part of the Flannery O'Connor Collection, located in the Ina

Dillard Russell Library, Georgia College, Milledgeville, Georgia; I am grateful for the assistance of Gerald Becham who was, for twelve years until 1982, Assistant Director of the Library and Curator of the O'Connor Collection.
16. Hans W. Frei, *The Identity of Jesus Christ: The Hermeneutical Bases of Dogmatic Theology* (Philadelphia: Fortress Press, 1975), 80–84.
17. Ibid., 83.

CHAPTER 8

1. Ruth Laney, "Conversation with Ernest J. Gaines: Interview," *Southern Review* 10 (January 1974): 3; see also Forrest Ingram and Barbara Steinberg, "On the Verge: An Interview with Ernest J. Gaines," *New Orleans Review* 3 (1973): 340.
2. Ingram and Steinberg, "On the Verge," 340.
3. Ernest J. Gaines, *The Autobiography of Miss Jane Pittman* (New York: Dial Press, 1971; New York: Bantam Books, 1972). In addition to the works cited in this chapter, Gaines has written four novels: *Catherine Carmier* (Chatham, N.J.: Chatham Bookseller, 1964); *Of Love and Dust* (1967; reprint, New York: W. W. Norton, 1979); *In My Father's House* (New York: Alfred A. Knopf, 1978); and *A Gathering of Old Men* (New York: Alfred A. Knopf, 1983).
4. Cf. Vilma Raskin Potter, "*The Autobiography of Miss Jane Pittman:* How to Make a White Film from a Black Novel," *Literature/Film Quarterly* 3 (Fall 1975): 371–75; and John Callahan, "Image-Making: Tradition and the Two Versions of Miss Jane Pittman," *Chicago Review* 29 (Autumn 1977): 45–62.
5. Gaines, *Autobiography*, vi.
6. Ibid., viii.
7. Ernest J. Gaines, *Bloodline* (New York: Dial Press, 1968). All further references to this work appear in the text.
8. Cf. an excellent discussion of the story by Barbara Puschmann-Nalenz, "Ernest J. Gaines: 'A Long Day in November,' " in *The Black American Short Story in the Twentieth Century: A Collection of Critical Essays*, ed. Peter Bruck (Amsterdam: B. R. Grüner Publishing Co., 1977), 157–69. See also Frank W. Shelton, "Ambiguous Manhood in Ernest J. Gaines's *Bloodline*," *CLAJ* 19 (December 1975): 200–209; Walter R. McDonald, " 'You Not a Bum, You a Man': Ernest J. Gaines's *Bloodline*," *Negro American Literary Forum* 9 (Summer 1975): 47–49; Jerry H. Bryant, "From Death to Life: The Fiction of Ernest J. Gaines," *Iowa Review* 3 (1972): 106–20.
9. Cf. Bryant, "From Death to Life," 107–8; Laney, "Conversation," 8–10; John O'Brien, ed., *Interviews with Black Writers* (New York: Liveright, 1973), 82. Another major influence Gaines consistently notes is that of William Faulkner.
10. Note Puschmann-Nalenz's analysis in "Ernest J. Gaines," especially 160–63.
11. Gaines acknowledges that he satirizes Christianity in some stories because as an institution the church has been resistant to change, at least in the days when his first stories were written, before the church's involvement in the civil rights movement. Cf. O'Brien, *Interviews with Black Writers*, 92. For other comments on religion, see Ingram and Steinberg, "On the Verge," 343.
12. O'Brien, *Interviews with Black Writers*, 91–92.
13. Ingram and Steinberg, "On the Verge," 342.
14. Ibid., 340.
15. Cf. especially McDonald, " 'You Not a Bum,' " 47–49; Puschmann-

Nalenz, "Ernest J. Gaines," 158–59, 163–66; and Shelton, "Ambiguous Manhood," 200.

16. Bryant, "From Death to Life," 112.

17. Paul Tillich, *Dynamics of Faith* (New York: Harper & Brothers, 1957), 1–8.

CHAPTER 9

1. Alice Walker, "The Black Writer and the Southern Experience," in *In Search of our Mothers' Gardens: Womanist Prose* (New York: Harcourt Brace Jovanovich, 1983), 17. This essay first appeared in *New South* 25 (Fall 1970): 23–26, and along with other material cited in this chapter has been included in Walker's recent collection of essays, hereafter referred to as *Mothers' Gardens*.

2. O'Brien, *Interviews with Black Writers,* 192; this interview is also included in *Mothers' Gardens,* 250.

3. Walker, "Beyond the Peacock: The Reconstruction of Flannery O'Connor," *Mothers' Gardens,* 52.

4. Ibid.

5. O'Brien, *Interviews with Black Writers,* 205; Walker, *Mothers' Gardens,* 265.

6. Walker, "The Black Writer," 17–18.

7. Walker, "In Search of our Mothers' Gardens," *Mothers' Gardens,* 233.

8. Ibid., 241.

9. Mary Helen Washington, "Teaching *Black-Eyed Susans*: An Approach to the Study of Black Women Writers," *BALF* 11 (Spring 1977): 20–24.

10. Martha J. McGowan, "Atonement and Release in Alice Walker's *Meridian,*" *Critique* 23 (1981): 25.

11. Many critics have commented on this dimension of her work. See especially, Gloria Steinem, "Do You Know This Woman? She Knows You: A Profile of Alice Walker," *Ms.* 10 (June 1982): 35, 37, 89, 90, 92–94.

12. Alice Walker, *Revolutionary Petunias and Other Poems* (New York: Harcourt Brace Jovanovich, 1973).

13. Walker, *In Love & Trouble,* 81–87. All further references to this work appear in the text. This story has not received much critical attention, but one of the most helpful, though brief, analyses is Faith Pullin, "Landscapes of Reality: The Fiction of Contemporary Afro-American Women," in *Black Fiction: New Studies in the Afro-American Novel Since 1945,* ed. A. Robert Lee (New York: Barnes & Noble, 1980), 187–89.

CHAPTER 10

1. Price, *A Palpable God,* 27.

2. Cf. ibid., 26–28.

3. William Ray, "Conversations: Reynolds Price and William Ray," *Mississippi Valley College Bulletin* 9 (Fall 1976): 7–9, 14–15.

4. Georges Gary, "A Great Deal More: Une Interview de Reynolds Price," *Recherches Anglaises et Américaines* 9 (1976): 135.

5. For a listing of Price's works, see Ray A. Roberts, "Reynolds Price: A Bibliographical Checklist," *American Book Collector* 2 (July-August 1981): 15–23.

6. Ray, "Conversations," 77.

7. Reynolds Price, *The Names and Faces of Heroes* (New York: Atheneum, 1963). All further references to this work appear in the text. There has not yet

been much sustained criticism of the stories in this collection, beyond passing references in initial reviews and in general studies of Price's work. One longer and more substantive review is that by John W. Stevenson, "The Faces of Reynolds Price's Short Fiction," *Studies in Short Fiction* 3 (Spring 1966): 300–306. There has also been a dissertation which I have not examined but which seems to promise more detailed criticism: Daniel Frederick Daniel, "Within and Without a Region: The Fiction of Reynolds Price," Ph.D. diss., University of Wisconsin-Madison, 1977.

The first published book-length study of Price's work also has a few pages on "A Chain of Love": Constance Rooke, *Reynolds Price* (Boston: Twayne, 1983), 40–42.

8. Wallace Kaufman, "A Conversation with Reynolds Price," *Shenandoah* 17 (Summer 1966): 10–11.

9. Ray, "Conversations," 40.

10. Ibid., 69.

11. Constance Rooke, "On Women and His Own Work: An Interview with Reynolds Price," *Southern Review* 14 (Autumn 1978): 707.

12. Gary, "Une Interview," 154.

13. Rooke, "On Women," 706–7.

14. Gary, "Une Interview," 154.

15. See Karl Rahner, "Anonymous Christians," in his *Theological Investigations* 6, trans. Karl-H. and Boniface Kruger (Baltimore: Helicon Press, 1969), 390–98. For another brief reference to this concept, cf. Hans Küng, *On Being a Christian*, trans. Edward Quinn (New York: Pocket Books, 1978), 97–98.

16. Gary, "Une Interview," 147.

17. Kaufman, "A Conversation," 17.

18. Rooke, "On Women," 707.

19. Reynolds Price, *A Generous Man* (New York: Atheneum, 1966), 275.

20. Cf. Vos, *The Drama of Comedy*.

21. Ray, "Conversations," 17.

22. Price, *A Palpable God*; David Rhoads and Donald Michie, *Mark as Story: An Introduction to the Narrative of a Gospel* (Philadelphia: Fortress Press, 1982).

23. Price, *A Palpable God*, 11.

24. Ray, "Conversations," 18.

25. Price, *A Palpable God*, 14.

26. Gary, "Une Interview," 145.